International capital movements

International capital movements

Based on the Marshall Lectures
given at the University of Cambridge 1985

Charles P. Kindleberger

Ford International Professor Emeritus,
Massachusetts Institute of Technology
and
Visiting Sachar Professor of Economics,
Brandeis University

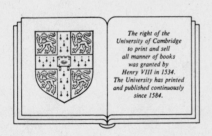

The right of the
University of Cambridge
to print and sell
all manner of books
was granted by
Henry VIII in 1534.
The University has printed
and published continuously
since 1584.

CAMBRIDGE UNIVERSITY PRESS

CAMBRIDGE
NEW YORK   NEW ROCHELLE
MELBOURNE   SYDNEY

Published by the Press Syndicate of the University of Cambridge
The Pitt Building, Trumpington Street, Cambridge CB2 1RP
32 East 57th Street, New York, NY 10022, USA
10 Stamford Road, Oakleigh, Melbourne 3166, Australia

First published 1987

Printed in Great Britain at the University Press, Cambridge

Reprinted 1988
First paperback edition 1988

British Library cataloguing in publication data

Kindleberger, Charles P.
International capital movements – based on
the Marshall Lectures given at the
University of Cambridge 1985.
1. Capital movements
I. Title
332'.042   HG3891

Library of Congress cataloguing in publication data

Kindleberger, Charles Poor, 1910–
International capital movements.
Includes index.
1. Capital movements. 2. Balance of payments.
3. Foreign exchange. 4. International finance.
I. Title
HG3891.K55 1987   332'.041   87–32733

ISBN 0 521 34132 9 hardcovers
ISBN 0 521 36984 3 paperback

WD

Contents

Preface

This book represents a considerable expansion of the 1985 Marshall Lectures in economics given at the University of Cambridge in November of that year. The occasion traditionally calls for two lectures on successive days, which would seem to be the maximum that a live audience should be subjected to. Expansion is called for partly to fill out passages where I was forced to condense during a lecture, and to add historical illustration. It is also needed to meet the minimum efficient size for publication in book form – an economic requirement that an economist tends to be respectful of. I have chosen to reorganize the material into four chapters, one on the balance of payments at the beginning, and another on financial deregulation and world capital market integration at the end, both, to be sure, very much concerned with capital movements, but keeping the descriptive portion of the lectures in the two central chapters on long- and short-term capital respectively.

I have also chosen to retain much of the original form of lecturing, with substantial use of the first-person singular pronoun, to keep something of the flavor of a lecture, perhaps, but also to lighten the task of revision. Subheadings have been added to give coherence and guidance. I trust the decision not to start over again and produce bite-size chapters of ten to fifteen pages will be tolerated in an older person, if not approved.

1 The balance of payments

Introduction

I am greatly honored to be invited to lecture in the distinguished series of lectures in memory of Alfred Marshall. I trust you will indulge me if I return to a subject of my youth – *à la recherche du temps perdu*, so to speak, or a return to the scene of the crime. My dissertation, published in 1937 – half a century ago – dealt with international short-term capital movements. Since that bygone era I have wandered more widely in international economics and economic history, without, however, entirely deserting the subjects of capital movements, foreign exchange, balances of payments and the like.

The gap of fifty years bothers me somewhat. My colleague, Paul Samuelson, has told me of reading an article a number of years ago by Professor Pigou, and thinking that it sounded familiar. He was, of course, certain that Pigou was not a plagiarist, but he was nonetheless curious as to its origin. Some digging revealed that it was similar to an article that had appeared fifty years earlier, written by Pigou himself. It seemed that certain synaps, long closed, had opened up again and Professor Pigou rediscovered his own theorem, analysis, conjecture, whatever it was. In these lectures I am acutely conscious of the fact that I repeat to a considerable extent what I have said on previous occasions.

International capital movements do not fit neatly into the thought of Alfred Marshall. The *Principles* (8th edn, 1920) refer to them not at all, as far as I see from a cursory view, perhaps because Marshall thought that little of first-rate importance remained to be worked out after the Bullion Report of 1810 (*Money, Credit and Commerce*, 1923 (1960), p. 135). The chapter on "International Exchanges" in *Money, Credit and Commerce* was said to be "an elementary account of matters that are familiar to every business man, and that are well understood by a great part of the general public" (ibid., p. 140). As indicated below, however, Marshall's discussion of international security markets has a very modern ring to it.

I choose to approach my subject with taxonomy, much as I did half a century ago. I shall first set out a few identities and definitional equations dealing with the balance of payments and its relationships with national income, though I shall use no mathematics, no econometrics, and none but the most casual empiricism. This is partly a matter of formation – the years when economics was being formalized were spent by me in government service and the Army. On returning to academic life I made the perhaps mistaken decision to carry on as a literary economist, interested in simple models and economic history. In part, however, I have come to believe that in order successfully to interpret what goes on in the real world it is necessary to change models continuously. I have insisted that this is true as between Keynesians on the one hand and monetarists on the other, between the analogous banking and currency schools in Britain in the first half of the nineteenth century – the latter thought by Marshall to have cleared our subject up – of the monetary and balance-of-payments explanations of the German inflation after World War I, and of such debates as to whether capital flows are correlated positively or negatively with the domestic business cycle (Kindleberger, 1985a). It is tempting to develop a single economic model for a given class of economic behavior and to cling to it. I believe it is a serious mistake and the analyst that relies on a single model is led deceptively into blind alleys.

The balance of payments

I start with an identity for the balance of payments

$$X - M - LTC - STC - G \equiv O \tag{1}$$

in which X stands for exports of goods and services; M is not money, as in most macro-economic discussion, but the absolute value of imports of goods and services; LTC are exports of long-term capital, with imports of capital having an implicit minus sign; STC are exports of short-term capital, imports again having an implicit negative sign; and G represents not government but imports of gold, with gold exports implicitly minus. I shall have something to say at a later stage about gold's recent transmutation from money into a commodity, but let me treat it for the nonce in a classical way.

Identity (1) says merely that the balance of payments always balances. It assumes perfect knowledge of transactions, so that there are no errors and no omissions. I further neglect for the time being such complications as transfers – foreign aid, reparations, indemnities and the like. I shall later break down various items, especially long-term capital (LTC) which is treated in chapter 2, and STC, the subject of chapter 3, into various subgroups with different characteristics. Observe that $X - M$ is the current account in the balance of payments, and that as a first approximation LTC and STC comprise the capital account and G the money account. In due course we shall find that much of STC belongs in the money account and that perhaps all of G should be counted among exports and imports of merchandise in the current account.

Early in the development of economics, little attention was paid to capital movements, although, as Postan reminded us, they were very much in evidence (1973). Bills of exchange assisted gold and silver in balancing exports and imports, a great improvement in efficiency as together they overcame the necessity to balance exports and imports in the very short run. Specie had gone some distance to meet the need for widening trade balances both in time and space, but the development of bills of exchange provided still greater freedom. The Hanseatic League, without bills of exchange, was limited to a kind of barter, selling goods abroad for local money then used to buy goods for import at the same time and the same place, except for small bilateral imbalances settled with specie (Dollinger, 1964 (1973)). But something like the fallacy of misplaced concreteness made early economists concentrate on exports, imports and specie. If LTC and STC drop out of identity (1) it becomes

$$X - M - G \equiv O \tag{1a}$$

David Hume insisted that equilibrium in the balance of payments of such a country was

$$X - M = O = G \tag{2}$$

This notion was developed in reaction to the mercantilists of the seventeenth and earlier centuries, who, with limited capital flows, wanted an export surplus on current account to accumulate specie. Their equilibrium position could be considered as

$$X - M = G \tag{3}$$

with both sides of the equation positive. Modern economics assumes that Hume's attack on the mercantilists revealed the fallacy of their thought. I have lately developed more sympathy with their position as I read of the "bullion famine" of the fifteenth century and up to about 1550, with specie drained to the Levant and the Eastern Baltic, areas that we would today regard as "low absorbers" (Day, 1978). Gold, silver and copper coin also disappeared through rubbing, sweating, clipping, wear and tear, and inadvertent loss, plus or minus the movement into or out of jewelry and plate. From time to time the shortage became so acute that it was necessary to substitute salt, pepper, cochineal (a dye) or similar valuable products traded at an arbitrary value for money, evoking in the economists of my immediate postwar generation the memory of the use of cigarettes, soluble coffee, and silk stockings for money in West Germany prior to the monetary reform of 1948. Mercantilists then were not completely stupid in their concern that a bullion famine might produce deflation. Theirs was a monetarist position, and one that differs from Keynes' view in *The General Theory* (1936, chap. 23) that the kernel of truth in mercantilism lay in the stimulus that exports gave to income and employment, a view that an expert on the period insists is inaccurate and riddled with misinterpretations (de Roover, 1949, p. 287n). In any event, by the eighteenth century, with the flow of specie from the New World distributed through bankrupt and indebted Spain to Genoa, Bruges, Antwerp, Amsterdam and London, mercantilist explanations were out of date and Hume's account of the price-specie-flow mechanism was needed. As a brief digression, I may observe that it often happens that economic analysis makes discontinuous changes in response to changes in the underlying situation. For a further, not unrelated example, note that physiocratic doctrine favoring the export of grain in place of a "policy of abundance" that restricted exports gained acceptance only when it was clear from the development of the grain trade from the Baltic to the Mediterranean that the populace would not have to rely completely on local supplies.

The transfer problem

When notice began to be taken of capital movements, the current account no longer served as the measure of an equilibrium position. The question now was whether the current account accommodated to the capital flow or perhaps vice versa. Most of *Money, Credit and Commerce* had been written in the 1890s before the treatment of the transfer problem by Taussig and his students, so that Marshall may be forgiven for thinking that little needed to be added to the Bullion Report of 1810.

The transfer problem came to the fore with the development of the accounting device of the balance of payments (Bullock, Williams and Tucker, 1919) and the problem posed by German reparations after World War I. There had been frequent indemnities before, in 1570, 1586, 1613 and the like, not to mention the classic cases of the indemnity paid by France with the help of a recycling Baring loan, to the allies victorious over Napoleon, and the Franco-Prussian indemnity of 1871–7 (Kindleberger, 1984, chap. xiii). Indeed, in the early sixteenth century loans were made and repaid in kind, including such commodities as copper and butter to illustrate the possibility (and the inefficiency) of the "natural" as opposed to the money economy (Heckscher, 1931 (1953), pp. 213–14). But the problem posed by the payment of reparations by Germany to the Allies after World War I faced economics squarely with the need to analyze transfers. The transfer problem arose because

$$X - M - LTC \neq O \neq STC + G \qquad (4a)$$

whereas equilibrium consisted in

$$X - M - LTC = O = STC + G \qquad (4b)$$

This latter definitional equation is referred to today as "basic balance" in international payments. Some of you may prefer to think of the autonomous items on the left-hand side as "above the line," and those on the right as "induced" and "below the line." You will, I hope, forgive me if I use this form of notation to emphasize that items can be shifted from autonomous to induced as the analysis of particular events requires. I suffered when the editor of the International Finance Section of Princeton University some years ago, the late Fritz Machlup, insisted on my changing the horizontal arrangement to a vertical one with the "line" where the equal signs come. I changed back when I escaped that determined editor.

You will recall that Viner believed that the movement of capital from London to Canada from 1896, and especially 1904, to 1913 was autonomous and the current account induced. He also thought that money movements served as instrumental variables and were reversed during the process as a whole (1924). In his model, the price-specie-flow mechanism brought it about that gold moved from Britain to Canada in the early part of the process to start the development of a goods surplus, and then reversed itself. The position ended up with the capital transferred in kind, the gold flows cancelled out and

$$LTC = X - M \qquad (5a)$$

R. H. Coats, the Canadian Dominion statistician, on the other hand thought the causation ran the other way – from expansion in Canada to an import surplus and an increase in interest rates that induced the capital flow (Board of Inquiry, 1915), in short

$$X - M = LTC \qquad (5b)$$

In Keynes' famous remark, capital was fluid and the current account "the sticky mass" (1929). Viner (1952) and Machlup (1950 (1964)) disagreed, contending that the current account is highly malleable and readily conformed to whatever direction and amount of capital might be forthcoming. They cited as example the experience of Germany continuing to pay reparations to the Allies after the inflow of private funds to Germany had halted in mid-1928, developing an export surplus to produce the foreign exchange needed to pay reparations, even in the depressed circumstances of 1930 and the first half of 1931. This was, however, at a tremendous social cost of 15 percent unemployment and the rise of the National Socialists to power. In 1958 in an article entitled "Equilibrium and Disequilibrium: Misplaced Concreteness and Disguised Politics," Machlup insisted that equilibrium in the balance of payments was a purely economic concept without political content. When the article was republished, he added a footnote saying that he had not meant to accuse Ragnar Nurkse (1949) or me, whose work had been cited in the article, of concealing or disguising the political dimensions of equilibrium when we had in fact been explicit on the point (1969, p. 128, n. 19). Toward the end of his life, Machlup recanted his earlier views entirely, and admitted that to transfer capital flight or reparations abroad through rigorous deflation might put such a severe strain on an economy as to jeopardize social and political stability.

National income and the balance of payments

The relationship of domestic investment to the balance of payments, of course, comes from the Alexander classic article (1952) in which he relates the balance of payments to what he calls "absorption." Starting with the definitional identity for national income (Y)

$$Y \equiv C + I + G \tag{6}$$

C being consumption, I investment and G government (not in this instance gold, but the meaning should always be clear in context), investment is broken down into segments, domestic and foreign

$$I = I_d + I_f \tag{6a}$$

I_f, that may be positive or negative, is the international movement of capital and money, or the current-account surplus or deficit.

Substituting and rearranging, one arrives at

$$X - M = Y - (C + I_d + G) \tag{6b}$$

which in equilibrium is the same, with the help of (5a), as

$$Y - (C + I_d + G) = LTC \tag{6c}$$

If absorption is less than national income, the surplus is taken off in long-term capital exports. In the Canadian case of Coats' showing, however, absorption exceeded income so that capital imports were induced. Alternatively, one can deal with savings and investment on a net basis, starting with $S = I_d + X - M$, and arrive at the net equivalent of (6c)

$$S - I_d = LTC \tag{6d}$$

In some cases it helps to break down savings into personal, corporate and government savings (surplus or deficit) $(S_p, S_c$ and $S_g)$. If one nets the corporate sector $(I_d$ and $S_c)$, (6d) becomes

$$S_p - (I_d - S_c) + S_g = LTC \tag{6e}$$

With corporate savings after net investment negative and offset by savings of the household sector, a government deficit produces a capital inflow. This is the position in the United States today.

Whether the government deficit crowds out domestic investment, raises interest rates that induce a capital flow that gives rise to the inward real transfer of capital – the current-account deficit – or the current-account deficit comes directly from the excess government spending that in turn leads to the capital inflow, or some of each, is a matter far from resolution by the most sophisticated statistical methods. In addition to the spending and interest-rate changes motivating capital flows, there are, in today's world, exchange-rate fluctuations giving rise to price changes and the responses to them of spending units, choosing between home and foreign-trade goods, and domestic and foreign assets. The ambiguities involved will be encountered below again and again. As already suggested, however, it is methodological error to insist that only one model is at work all the time, or even in a given complex incident. Here, as in Marshall's famous general-equilibrium example of balls in a bowl, the position of each determines the position of all others and vice versa.

What this means, of course, is that it is a mistake to lay all the blame for the United States deficit vis-à-vis Japan on the U.S. governmental budget deficit ($S_g < O$) or on high Japanese personal savings ($S_p > O$), explaining the former, say, by rising entitlements under the social security laws passed in president Roosevelt's time with indexation, farm subsidies, and President Reagan's commitments to high defense expenditure and to no turning back from the tax reductions made early in his first term; ascribing the latter to Japan's lack of social security provision at the national level, forcing each family to save for its own retirement, to the payment of salaries thirteen times a year with the annual bonus of a month's pay that tends to be saved, and the like. In equilibrium, everything determines everything.

In this discussion of net investment or net savings and long-term capital flows, it is assumed that the money variables cancel out in the transfer process, i.e., that the gold and/or short-term capital flow is reversed when transfer is complete. But Jeffrey Williamson, in treating the history of the American balance of payments in the nineteenth century, made a crucial contribution to the discussion that is generally overlooked (1964). The transfer mechanism in the typical analysis, he stated, assumes that the movement of long-term capital is balanced by the net of exports and imports of goods and services. Given growth, however, a country's money stock must grow. It can acquire more money by an export of goods and services. It can equally do so by borrowing. In the nineteenth century, the United States borrowed abroad mainly to acquire goods and services for capital investment, but partly also to enlarge the money stock. This money was not an instrument but part of the purpose of borrowing. This is international financial intermediation, borrowing long and holding gold. We shall hear more of international financial intermediation, perhaps more than you will want to hear.

In Williamson's version, three markets must clear in equilibrium – not separately but in the aggregate – that for goods and services ($X - M$), that for financial assets and to some degree real capital (LTC), and that for money ($STC + G$). The monetarist view of the balance of payments acknowledges that the money stock must grow with economic development but again assumes only two markets, for money and for goods. With more money needed as growth proceeds, the country must develop an export surplus. But with three markets in overall balance, that is no longer necessary. The sought-after money can be borrowed. And unlike the Viner model of the transfer process with the price-specie-flow mechanism at work, it need not return. In fact the distribution of new supplies of specie from the gold and silver mines of Europe, Africa and the New World took place partly through the trade account but also through capital movements.

Let us, however, dispense with gold for the time being. Since at least 1971 when the United States closed the gold window, or perhaps 1968 when the gold pool in London broke up and the two-tier price system was introduced, gold has been a commodity rather than money. The Midas neurosis, or perhaps I should say "paranoia," still abounds, not least in central banks. The nostalgia for a return to the gold standard evident in France and in the small band of American followers of Jacques Rueff and Robert Mundell in the United States seems doomed to frustration, especially after the Reagan Gold Commission's negative report written by Anna Jacobson Schwartz, rejecting a return to the gold standard in favor of monetarism. Unable now to serve as a medium of exchange or unit of account, gold is no longer international money. It has lost the unit-of-account function because of its varying price, when the moneyness of money rests in the fact that its price is constant in terms of other monies. I shall occasionally reintroduce gold into these definitions to conform to classical definitions, but the principal international money is short-term capital, in an earlier day sterling, today usually dollars.

The three markets that have to clear: for goods and services, for long-term assets or liabilities, and for money, conform to three modes of analysis in balances of payments: the elasticities and/or absorption, the absorption, and the monetary. The monetary approach assumes that exports and imports of goods and services adjust to the relationship between the demand for and the supply of money in a given country. I lack an intuitive feel for this, since I normally think of money as balancing the difference between income and expenditure through time, rather than expenditure and income adjusting to the net demand for money. In addition, one can obtain money by borrowing – financial intermediation. But all three approaches are needed: no single model of the balance of payments is good for all times and places. The economist with but one model for the analysis of the balance of payments has handicapped him- or herself. It would be absurd, for example, to explain the Saudi Arabian balance-of-payments surplus from 1974 to about 1982 in terms of a Keynesian or a monetarist model, to argue, for example, that after the sharp increases in the price of oil, that country had a high propensity to save and low investment, or experienced a sudden increase in its demand for money. This was an elasticities case, with the elasticities failing to pass the Marshall-Lerner test, a case, that is, based on elasticity pessimism (in the short run). Concurrently, balance-of-payments surpluses of the Federal Republic of Germany and Japan follow the absorption model. I shall waffle between the absorption model based on the government deficit, and the elasticities model responding with high elasticities to the appreciation of the dollar in explaining the present U.S. payments deficit. In the long run, of course, the three models – elasticities, absorption and monetary – converge. In the short run one or another of them drives the adjustment process. It is not always obvious which. The choice requires economic instinct, or intuition, more often than economic measurement, and especially more than number-crunching to find the best R square.

Equally in the transfer case, sometimes capital drives the current account, sometimes the other way round. I have referred to the debate between Viner and Coats; in the constant re-examination of the Canadian case, the weight of opinion has come solidly down on the Coats' side to conclude that the boom in Canada attracted the capital, rather than the capital produced the boom. In 1885 in London, anticipating the Goschen conversion that brought the yield on consols down from 3 to 2½ percent, there was a surge of capital abroad in search of higher income, a backward-bending supply curve, if you like, or target-worker model. "John Bull can stand many things but he can't stand two percent." The *rentier*'s income target can be met either by taking greater risk to earn the same gross income, or through saving more at the lower interest rates. In either instance, foreign lending is likely to be increased. There were, to be sure, discoveries of diamonds and gold in South Africa, or nitrates in Chile, the opening of new lands in Argentina, and the building of cities after the completion of the railroads in Australia. History is replete with "stories" of sudden changes in financial markets followed by capital outflow; the success of the Baring loan to finance the French indemnity in 1817, the conversion of the British war debt in 1822, enormous oversubscriptions to the Thiers *rentes* in 1871 and 1872, and the unexpected success of the American tranche of the Dawes loan in 1924. And in these cases, the capital flow leads to changes in the current account that brings about the real transfer. That was not the case, however, in the classic Canadian borrowing when the boom produced the capital inflow.

It is sometimes difficult to decide which is the autonomous element in the balance of payments and which the induced. Such a time is the world of today, with some part of the capital flow to the United States induced by the high interest rates that resulted from the governmental budget deficit, some part autonomous as European investors sought dollars and investments away from the troubles of Europe and the Middle East. In these cases theory is less interesting than historical description.

2 Long-term capital

The taxonomy

Back to our taxonomy, and for long-term capital rather than balance-of-payments models. Long- is ordinarily distinguished from short-term capital by the nature of the financial instrument, with long-term capital operating through equities and debt instruments of more than a year's maturity. There is, of course, a problem that instruments may not be congruent with function: one can move into and out of equities in months, weeks or days, whereas investments in short maturities can be rolled over many times to constitute an effective long-term investment.

The usual division of long-term capital is into new issues, trade in existing securities, both bonds and shares, and direct foreign investment. This last is ownership of real assets or of an equity position in a company that gives the foreign owner control. The behavior of each of these three forms of long-term investment differs both as a rule, and again, on occasion, at different times and different places. Changes in these forms of behavior have been shaped by changes in the economic environment, notably by improvements in international transport and communication. The different forms also require different modes of analysis. New security issues, for example, tend to fit flow models, with excesses of savings in one or more countries available for investment in countries where investment demands exceed savings. At the same time, trade in existing securities fits rather a portfolio model, in which investors rearrange portfolios in response to parametric changes.

Too much must not be made of the need for different models for different forms of international investment. Over time, of course, the flow model and the portfolio model converge, as flows build up or reduce holdings which are then adjusted from time to time. It is true that the flow model fits lending between developed and underdeveloped countries and the portfolio model that among financially developed countries with their opportunities for diversification and responses to changes in interest rates, exchange rates and business prospects. But it is important to underline that new issues and trade in existing securities are intimately related.

A new work by Christopher Platt makes the important point that most tabulations of foreign long-term lending overstate the capital flows, since investors in a borrowing country frequently buy a large portion of the bonds issues abroad by their national governmental and private bodies (1984). It has long been known, for example, that European investors after World War II bought up a large proportion of the bonds issued by European borrowers in New York (Kindleberger, 1963 (1966), pp. 72–5). Platt is insisting that developing countries must basically rely on their own resources, and notes that the phenomenon is not new. During the 1840s, French railroad securities issued in London were bought mainly by French investors. The German purchases of Italian bank stocks after 1894 that Gerschenkron made so much of (1962, pp. 87–9) were in 1900 mostly back in Italian hands (Confalonieri, 1967, iii, pp. 3–17). J. W. Beyen stated that it was typical for Holland in the inter-war period to float government loans in New York to cover its internal government deficit – it had no interest in acquiring foreign exchange – and to find that the loans had been almost totally "repatriated" within a year of their issue (1949, p. 13). In the French case, as Platt points out, and equally in many instances such as Argentine investors buying Argentine securities floated in Europe, the foreign underwriters are intermediating between two parties in the borrowing country. In addition, the lenders in the borrowing country are prepared to accept a lower return than available at home because they get a better security – one with a wider market and hence greater liquidity – and one on which the local borrower may be less willing to default because of international complications. Bringing demand

and supply both from a smaller to a larger financial center is a superior process to merely matching the excess demand for savings in one with the net excess of supply in the other. Economies of scale in the broadened market create a different, better, and hence cheaper kind of security.

It is, by the way, not universally true that gross flows are many times net, although this is surely truer today than it has been in the past as we shall see below in stressing financial intermediation (see also Wallich, 1984a). Viner's estimates of the capital movement from London to Canada made no allowance for Canadian purchases of Canadian securities in London (1924, chap. vi), and Hall, writing about the capital movement from Britain to Australia, mentions Australian banks holding British government securities as reserves, but has no word of Australian savers buying Australian securities issued in London (1963, p. 51). It may be that Commonwealth savers were at the same time Commonwealth investors – investing directly with greater animal spirits as Keynes would have said, more entrepreneurial and less interested in assured *rentier* income. If so, this would make them less interested in the interposition of intermediaries between their money and their primary investment. But this is a weak ad hoc hypothesis, and the question awaits detailed research to explain the difference between, say, Argentine investment practice and that of Australia and Canada.

New securities normally flow in channels, rather than spreading evenly over the earth as a whole. Investors typically scan limited horizons because of positive information costs. These horizons may expand or contract in response to events. The stimuli to foreign lending from the Baring indemnity loan, the Thiers *rentes*, Dawes loan, and the 1822 and 1888 debt conversions have been mentioned. Negative as well as positive horizon shifts have occurred. The Fourth Anglo-Dutch war in 1780 caused the Dutch to shift their lending from Britain to France. London turned away from the Continent as a consequence of the revolutions of 1848, redirecting savings to the Dominions, the Empire and Egypt. Simultaneous massive shifts occurred in 1887 when the Germans stopped lending to Czarist Russia, and the French started. Political tension between

Germany and Russia coincided with a domestic boom that made the Germans anxious to bring capital home for investment, and with a surge of lending by the French, still exhilarated by the spectacular rise of the Thiers *rentes*. In effect, Russia recycled its debt from Germany to France and Parisian capital went through St Petersburg to Berlin. A more modern and negative illustration of a shift of horizons was the start of the stock-market boom in the second quarter of 1928 that made New York investors divert their attention away from the lending to Germany and the developing countries that had so thoroughly beguiled them since 1924.

Canada has traditionally held a different status in the New York market than other foreign borrowers, because of its shared border with the United States, and its close cultural ties (albeit with some conscious distancing). In the minds of some investors, Canadian securities are not foreign at all: an insurance financial executive will insist in one breath that his company does not invest in foreign bonds, but admit in the next that it buys Canadian dominion and provincial issues. Or a manufacturing company such as Campbell Soup will assert that it had no foreign investment before World War II though of course it does manufacturing and marketing in Canada. Americans like to think of Canada as the thirteenth Federal Reserve district; Canadians are understandably less attracted to the remark. These blind spots are not unknown elsewhere in foreign investments: it may be merely a joke, in a book full of delightful anecdotes, but Emden tells the story of a Parisian investor who sought to buy Suez shares, thinking the company ran a railroad on an island in Sweden. When told that the company was constructing a canal between Egypt and Palestine, he said he did not care as long as the investment was anti-British (Emden, 1938, p. 309). The run that undid the Creditanstalt in Austria in May 1931 spread to German banks, some thought, because of the "fact" that American investors did not know the difference between the two countries (Bennett, 1962, p. 23).

Cyclical patterns

The cyclical pattern of long-term lending presents another of those cases where no one model predominates, but two alternate.

In a demand-led model, a given volume of savings is directed to home borrowers or abroad depending upon the rhythm of the domestic business cycle. In domestic boom, foreign lending slows down; in depression it speeds up. In a supply model, on the other hand, domestic and foreign investment fluctuate together as savings rise and fall in the course of the domestic business cycle. The point has long been made that British nineteenth-century lending was counter-cyclical, while American in the 1920s was procyclical. The difference was thought to be the result of accumulated experience in London, and inexperience in New York (Cairncross, 1953). There is much to this explanation. Especially when a horizon shift has just occurred and there are new unexploited opportunities for foreign lending, new loans will rise and fall with the availability of savings, whereas after lending with a fixed horizon has been underway for a time, the demand model predominates. These general tendencies cannot be used, however, to predict; British lending was procyclical in the second half of the 1880s, and again in 1910–13, and German foreign lending was counter-cyclical after 1873 when it first got started in buying foreign bonds in a big way.

There is a temptation to suggest that long-term capital in new security issues flows from capital-abundant to capital-scarce countries, and, with allowance made for intermediation by under-writers abroad between domestic borrowers and lenders, this is the case. In trade in existing securities the capital flows are less uni-directional. Diversification is one motive. Canada is on balance a recipient of net capital flows from the United States, both through government securities and direct investment. On the other hand, Canadian investors hold a large portfolio of United States equities, including both blue chips – the seasoned securities of long successful companies – and high-flying growth companies. Canada from time to time has had considerable reservations about the welcome it should accord to foreign direct investment, but the suggestion that it should requisition private holdings of U.S. securities and use the dollar proceeds of their sale to buy out American interests in Canadian industry evoked a storm of protest in Canada. Access to a different type of security improves investor welfare even when he or she chooses not to take advantage of it.

The phenomenon is by no means confined to the investments of the United States in Canada and vice-versa. Observing the large gross claims among countries and the small net movement, Governor Henry Wallich of the Federal Reserve Board has conjectured that perhaps different rates of savings and investment in countries do not count for so much as do the diversification interests of asset holders and the marketing and production strategies of industrial corporations (1984a). Wallich's analysis covered direct investment as well as new issues and trading in outstanding securities, the former being a subject we have yet to deal with. It nonetheless suggests that one should be wary about over-explaining net movements when the gross in the opposite direction is substantial. While net capital movements may be small on balance, it is noteworthy that in a separate paper the same year, Wallich observes that international capital movements are "the tail that wags the dog," that is, that capital flows dominate the balance of payments and exchange-rate changes, despite their relatively small net size compared with exports and imports of goods and services in the current account of the balance of payments (1984b).

Trade in existing securities

Some trade in existing securities is based on differences in views about the prospects for given companies. Inexperienced financial journalists sometimes say that a given stock market went up because foreigners bought shares, or down because they sold them. This is solecistic: foreigners buy or sell domestic securities on balance as the market goes up or down, depending on the relative views of the two sets of traders. The market can go up when foreigners are net sellers, or down when they are net buyers; it may go down or up with no actual international transactions as foreign and domestic traders revise their views of appropriate prices in the same direction and to the same extent.

An outstanding instance of differences in views is recorded just before the Baring 1890 crisis when German investors in Argentine *cedulas* (mortgages) and Argentine sterling bonds dumped them in London, whether because of the cautiousness of German investors and the hostility of the German government (Ferns, 1960, pp. x, 433; Lauck, 1907, pp. 59–60), or because of specific concern for the depreciation of the peso (Morgenstern, 1959, p. 523). Later in the same crisis, British investors sold off American securities to add to their liquidity, first in Paris (Théry, quoted in Morgenstern, ibid., p. 526), and then, followed by Paris and Berlin investors, in New York (Simon, 1955 (1978), pp. 454, 473, 501).

International trade in outstanding securities may be entirely local insofar as the investors are concerned, with the two markets joined by arbitrageurs who buy in one market and simultaneously sell in the other. If Dutch investors have a higher regard for General Motors than New York investors, arbitrageurs will buy stock in New York and sell it in Amsterdam, moving capital for the purpose from the Netherlands to the United States. I understood at the time, perhaps with inadequate information, that British foreign-exchange control immediately after World War II and before the ill-fated convertibility called for by the Anglo-American Financial Agreement had a grave leak in permitted arbitrage in Kaffirs. British capitalists, if the story is correct, bought Kaffirs in London and sold them in Johannesburg. If arbitrage had been prohibited, the movement would have quickly come to an end as Kaffirs rose in price in London, and fell in Johannesburg, to reflect the implicit discount on sterling. With arbitrage permitted, however, whether through inadvertence or misunderstanding, the Bank of England permitted a massive capital outflow as professional arbitrageurs were accorded foreign exchange to equalize prices by buying in South Africa and selling in England.

Marshall made the point that with first-class exportable securities, importers in case of need can pay by this means, or exporters receive payment (1923, p. 151). In discussing the Puerto Rican balance of payments, James C. Ingram described a system by which the island settled its net payments or receipts with the mainland in U.S. government bonds (1959). This, of course, is using a long-term instrument as if it were short-term, i.e., as money. Whether there are many securities that can fill such a role today beyond U.S. governments and a few blue-chip equities such as the shares of A.E.G., Exxon, Ford, General Motors, Phillips, Schlumberger, Shell, Siemens and the like is doubtful, although the numbers involved are doubtless increasing. In these cases, an element of *LTC* should be dealt with on the right-hand side of the equations defining equilibrium, as if it were *STC*.

Speculative flows

Long-term capital can be a conduit to transfer savings abroad in a flow, it can serve as a means of adjusting capital stocks to changes in circumstances, and it can be used as money. It is also a subject for speculation, resulting in occasional instability. A number of economists with strong views about the efficiency of markets maintain that destabilizing speculation is impossible. The argument runs that if one buys as prices rise and sells as prices fall one is bound to lose money and suffer Darwinian extinction. Destabilizing speculation seems to be found in economic history, along with the stabilizing variety, if not in all brands of economic theory. Rational expectations and those who deny the possibility of destabilizing speculations appear to consider markets as made up of identical actors with the same information, the same intelligence, viewpoint and motivation, whereas a moderately close reading of history suggests differences along these several lines. In early canal companies in Britain, for example, one class of investors consisted of investors along the right of way who were interested in promoting the canal for its effect on their other more direct interests, e.g., Bolton and Watt in Birmingham or Wedgwood in nearby Soho, who wanted cheap and reliable transport for their inputs and outputs. Another set of investors was made up of persons looking for a long-term outlet for savings. Both these groups bought canal shares to hold. A third class consisted of alert and sophisticated speculators who observed the profitability of the investment and the rise in its shares. They invested for capital gains, buying in the hope of selling later at a profit. Their purchases were often leveraged by delayed payment of their subscriptions or by use of borrowed funds. Still a fourth class consisted of ignorant investors, who late in the day caught on to the profits made by the third group. As Jefferys points out about domestic investment in Britain, the denomination of shares was brought steadily down from £100 or £200 to £50, £25, £10 or £5, and even in some cases to 10s. to widen the catchment basis to include "servant girls and greengrocers" (1946 (1954), p. 53), or as we would say in the United States "waiters and bootblacks." These last classes were presumably enticed more readily by domestic shares than by the issue of foreign bonds, but their unsophisticated equivalent investing in foreign securities has often been described as widows and orphans, plus perhaps retired persons, civil servants and the like (Kindleberger, 1978, p. 31n).

A great deal of research on aspects of macro-economic questions concerns rational expectations. Theorists assert that rationality is required as an axiom in economies either because it is impossible to reason if one thinks of the world as irrational, or because the mathematics of irrationality are too complex to be handled. I have a footnote in a paper on bank failures suggesting that it seems more useful to appeal to history in deciding whether the world is uniformly rational, uniformly irrational, or generally rational but occasionally irrational (Kindleberger, 1985, p. 31).

The investors who bought foreign government and railroad bonds issued by such debtors as Argentina, Czarist Russia or the southern states of the United States during the War Between the States thought they were behaving rationally. They reasoned from the safety of government and railroad securities in Western Europe to the safety of government and railroad bonds everywhere. *Ex post* this extrapolation seems simple-minded rather than irrational, but the distinction is difficult to draw.

On the other hand, one can find instances where borrowers and lenders behaved rationally in complex circumstances that would seem to defeat all but the most sophisticated financial experts. I have in mind the Gibson paradox, or more generally the Fisher effect, that suggests that when prices are rising lenders insist on higher rates of interest because they expect to be repaid in depreciated monies, while when prices are falling, borrowers insist on very low rates of interest because they expect to have to pay back their loans in more valuable money. At one stage, Robert Mundell hypothesized that some international lending and borrowing took place because of a sort of "exchange illusion," comparable to "money illusion" in a domestic economy, that confused nominal money transactions with those in real terms, i.e., money amounts deflated by changes in the price level. He thought, for example, that in an inflationary period, international lenders would charge too little so that it would pay to borrow heavily and pay back with depreciated currency (Mundell, 1968). Casual empiricism suggests that this has happened in a number of cases, e.g., the German inflation after World War I and Latin American inflations after World War II. Two careful historical studies, however, suggest that neither borrowers nor lenders in the past have succumbed to exchange illusion. Lenders in Britain did not fail to understand the relation of price changes to interest rates (Harley, 1977), and the borrowing Czarist government, a sophisticated econometric study shows, did not overborrow during the Great Depression from 1873 to 1896 because of being misled by falling prices (Israelsen, 1979). French and German investors were taken in by venal and corrupt journalists, who hawked securities in the press against bribes, like payola disk-jockeys of a few years ago (Stern, 1977, chap. 11; Bouvier, 1960), but if the econometrics is credible, they did not fail to distinguish real from nominal interest rates. The issue of course is more complex under flexible exchange rates. I touch on this on p. 32.

The speculative model applies not only to new issues, but also to trade in outstanding issues, and even in foreign exchange. A "displacement" or autonomous perturbation occurs. Prices change, and with them new profit opportunities are opened up. It may happen that a wave of euphoria follows. Credit is monetized. With delay between the start of the new investment and its ultimate output, prices rise further. In the course of time, the elastic expectations of rising prices and burgeoning profits erode, as far-sighted investors pull back. With expectations in process of reversing, markets are in "distress." Slowly or quickly they may be reversed, possibly leading to a collapse.

A classic case in foreign lending is provided by the 1885 to 1890 boom. Euphoric expectations spread across the world from South Africa to Latin America, Australia and the United States. A boom in brewery shares spread from London to Canada and the United States. European stock markets were infected by the 1928–9 boom on Wall Street. In the 1950s and 1960s, investment trusts were formed in New York to participate in the boom in German and Japanese shares.

Perhaps the outstanding instance of international speculation – of a stabilizing character as it happened – was that of the Thiers *rentes*, issued in 1871 and 1872, as France sought to raise the 5-billion-franc indemnity to pay to Prussia to rid the country of military occupation. The first *rente*, issued in July 1871, was for 2½ billion, and priced at 82.50 francs for a 100-franc bond, with denominations as low as five francs. It was twice oversubscribed, with 1,135 millions coming from abroad, including some bids from as far away as India. The *rente* rose rapidly in price to almost 95 by October. The second *rente* issued in July 1872 was for 3 billion francs, priced at 84.50 francs and oversubscribed thirteen times. Berlin alone bid for 3 billions' worth, and Berlin and North Germany together 4½ billion. These sums were not serious, of course, as investors, including, especially, banks, bid to acquire *rentes* which they expected to sell when the price rose. French investors selling foreign securities to buy the *rente*, and foreign purchasers together provided the foreign exchange needed to meet the indemnity.

This was a recycling operation *par excellence*. The real transfer occurred when the foreign investors sold their *rentes* to return to their normal investment habitat, and French investors rebuilt their foreign portfolios. This enormous operation (for its time) worked smoothly in stable fashion. Other surges of foreign lending which were sharply reversed – the 1885 surge from London cut off by the Baring collapse of November 1890, or the New York foreign-lending burst following the Dawes loan which subsided suddenly in the middle of 1928 when the stock-market boom got under way – destabilized the world economy like a game of snap-the-whip played by children.

Foreign direct investment

Foreign direct investment may take the form of purchases of securities in a foreign corporation, existing or formed for the purpose, but its essence is control. Control is sought for the purpose of squeezing all the rent, in a Ricardian sense, out of a given advantage, often one in technology, sometimes in the capacity of a vertically integrated company, stretching across national boundaries, to coordinate separate stages of production and distribution more effectively than the atomistic competitive market can. Stephen Hymer is credited with the major development in the theory of foreign direct investment when he observed that the subject belongs less to the theory of international capital movements than to industrial organization (1960, 1976). There is little foreign direct investment in competitive industries. Unlike lending through securities, where apart from diversification, savings normally flow from capital-rich to capital-poor countries, direct investment flows both ways, often in the same industries. Interpreted in terms of the formula for capitalizing a stream of income:

$$C = \frac{I}{r}$$

where C is the capitalized value of an earning asset, I is the stream of income produced, and r is the competitive rate of return, Hymer suggested that direct investment moves because of higher rates of return, I, based on a company's advantage, rather than on national differences in r.

Like lending through securities, direct investment responds to changes in horizons. The geographical area of its operations that can be managed effectively by a company depends upon the costs of transport and communications. Apart from banking, and I suppose a few exceptions such as the Vatican, the Hanseatic League, the chartered companies, foreign direct investment became significant in the middle of the nineteenth century with the advent of the steamship and the telegraph, and took a major upward leap with the arrival of the jet aircraft and transoceanic telephone. American firms responded to the Rome treaty of 1957, I conjecture, less because of the changed investment opportunities produced by the customs union than because it drew their attention to existing opportunities that had lain unnoticed beyond their horizons. Not everyone subscribes to this theory of direct investment. Robert Aliber, for example, maintains that the strongest currency affords companies in its area an advantage in investing over others in weaker currencies, because of investor preference for securities denominated in the strong currency and hence a cheaper cost of capital, so that the theory of direct investment should be linked to countries, not companies in particular industries (1970, 1983). He tries to explain cross investment in given industries – Exxon in Britain and Shell in the United States, or Lever Brothers in the U.S. and Proctor and Gamble in the U.K. – on successive waves of investment as currencies wax and wane in strength, as contrasted with the industrial-organization view that cross investment represents an exchange of threats. In that view a company invests in its competitor's back yard to warn the latter not to make trouble in the investor's primary market, if it wants to lead a quiet life and escape retaliation. This sort of direct investment conforms to a model of defensive strategy.

Defensive investment occurs rather widely in foreign direct investment. The concept was developed by Alexander Lamfalussy, then in academic life, now the Managing Director of the Bank for International Settlements, who observed some years after World War II that the Belgian textile industry was investing at a rapid clip, but failing to earn a normal return for Belgian firms (1961). After digging into the matter he concluded that the industry had to run fast to stay in the same place. Without high investment it would have lost, say, 6 percent per annum. Investing heavily, it was earning 2 percent a year gross, or 8 percent as compared with what the position would have been without making the investment. In this instance, to be sure, defensive investment was a short-run device only.

In foreign direct investment, defensive investment takes place in markets where the return is not as high as the firm's normal rate of profit, but it is undertaken to forestall losses elsewhere. A company will enter a certain market at less than its normal return to prevent a competitor from making a killing that would position it to give trouble in the investing company's home market or in a third market. Or a New York bank will establish a branch in Paris, where it is difficult for foreign banks to compete, in order to avoid the possible loss of a client from New York who goes to Paris and wants to deal with his usual bank. With meticulous cost accounting, the Paris branch could be credited with some of the earnings of the home office that were saved by the maintenance of a presence in that market (Koszul, 1970). Under ordinary accounting, head-office profits would be above normal, branch profits below normal, but the position is in equilibrium because of jointness. No such jointness occurs as a rule in security investments.

Jointness in direct investment can be extensive or limited, as it can be, for that matter, in any firm with a complex functional or geographic structure. One young economist thinks of the multinational corporation as a device for arbitraging capital, goods, technology and personnel (Kogut, 1983). To the extent that this is the case, the separate elements are linked in a sort of jointness. In other cases, the rule will be that "each tub must stand on its own bottom," i.e., be a profit center which earns as much as other profit centers. The question is whether a given multinational corporation is a single unit operating worldwide or has a more federal structure, as an agglomeration, that can be expanded or shrunk by buying or selling sub-units, without much affecting the totality (Kindleberger, 1985c). The "each-tub-on-its-own-bottom" model is close to zero-based budgeting in which the separate subsidiaries are expected to justify their continued existence each year (in the revolving corporate five-year capital budget, for example). The unitary approach assumes that each subsidiary goes on from year to year unless there is some substantial and unexpected change in its contribution to the total.

A difference between foreign direct investment and investment through security purchases similar to that in jointness comes from the fineness of some of the calculations made by companies undertaking direct investment. There is cross investment, as already noted. And there are industries where apparently similar companies behave in different ways, and also companies that change their minds, to suggest that the invest/don't-invest decision is often very close. In flat glass, the French St Gobain Company with a new process invested in new facilities in the United States, whereas the British Pilkington firm, with an even better new process decided initially to license the technology. Later Pilkington abandoned its earlier coyness and bought the automobile glass plants of Libbey-Owens-Ford. The same disparate behavior can be observed in automobiles: Volkswagen early bought the Studebaker assembly plant in Linden, New Jersey, changed its mind before it had begun operations, and sold it. Volvo planned a big assembly operation in a free-trade zone in Virginia, changed its mind, and abandoned the venture. Then Volkswagen changed its mind again, and started up production of its Golf model (in the United States called the Rabbit) in Altoona, Pennsylvania. The decision whether to build or export, build or license, turns on a wide variety of variables related to tariffs, technology, the behavior of competitors, available assistance and the like in which companies in slightly different circumstances, or the same company at different times, may emerge from the decision process with opposite results.

One could go on at length about foreign direct investment, as I did not in my 1937 dissertation but have done on more than one occasion since. One critical point may be made, however, in connection with capital movements. Sometimes direct investment involves very little in the way of new money raised in the home country and used to purchase the currency of the host. Initial investment may be made for some part in kind – perhaps patents, machinery, the cost of experts sent from the home office, etc. – and local borrowing for the rest. Much of growth has historically come from reinvested profits – part of the international balance of payments but not the balance of international payments, since no international payment is involved. During the 1930s, substantial investments were made in Germany by companies which were unable, because of foreign-exchange control, to get profits out. While foreign direct investment rightfully belongs to the theory of industrial organization, it is too much to say, as some have done, that it should be excluded from all discussion of capital movements, and confined, so far as capital is concerned, to capital formation. But the act of saving and the act of investment are much more closely tied, and the transfer problem is less in evidence in direct investment than in long-term direct flows through security markets, whether those for new issues or for outstanding stocks and bonds.

Let me offer a couple of other comparisons of direct investment and capital movements through securities, without a solid basis in statistical demonstration. First it is my strong impression that the cyclical pattern of direct investment clings fairly consistently to the supply model, rising in boom and subsiding, though not necessarily reversing itself, in recession, in contrast with security flows which sometimes follow the supply model that varies with the supply of savings, and sometimes the demand model allocating a given body of savings between home and foreign uses depending upon the relative demand conditions. Companies typically like to grow, and have plans for expansion which they seek to realize in periods when profits are high. They are, as a rule, fearful of paying out rising profits too rapidly to shareholders since the latter come to expect too much. When profits are high, therefore, they tend to expand both at home and abroad in the pro-cyclical pattern. At the same time, I think that a number of observers – Stephen Hymer (1960 (1976)), Harry Johnson (1971) and Albert Hirschman (1969) overstate the matter when they assert that foreign direct investment always grows and is never reversed. Hymer said that foreign direct investment resembles a long-lived tree, rather than an annual flower, and Johnson extended the metaphor by comparing it with the giant redwood that lasts for centuries. But it has happened frequently that a surge of direct investment is reversed when the investing firm finds a better use for the funds at home, or needs cash to make up losses. I observed that Germany on four occasions complained of *Überfremdung* – overforeignization, or too much foreign control of German mines and industry – in the 1850s, the 1890s, the 1920s and the 1950s – with the complaints dying down in each instance as a substantial portion of the investment was reversed (Kindleberger, 1978b, pp. 207–9). Multinational corporations with head offices in the United States have sold off part of their foreign holdings in the 1930s, and again in the recessions of 1974–5 and 1980–2, to acquire cash to make good losses at home.

Second, an important difference between debt and direct investment turns on the attitudes to them of less developed countries in periods of inflation and of recession. During the 1950s and 1960s, the Latin American countries especially were unhappy that foreign investors favored direct investment and were loath to buy Latin American bonds. In the 1970s and 1980s, the same countries have insisted that they preferred to receive foreign capital in the form of equity participations rather than as debt. But of course. Inflation wipes out debt, whereas foreign direct investment stays intact and profits soar. This explains investor preferences in the 1950s and 1960s and *LDC* opposition to direct investment then. On the other hand, direct investment earns little in recession whereas debt service is difficult to maintain because of shrinking exports. We all want it both ways. Circumstances alter cases. But one must be careful not to draw sweeping conclusions with unsustainable claims to generality.

Perfect international capital markets?

The Coase theorem states that institutions spring into place to meet economic needs. The Macmillan "gap" in Britain provides one counterexample, discovered only in 1931, but in existence earlier (Jefferys, 1938 (1977)). This was the gap in capacity to raise capital between small firms of less than £100,000 that relied on local resources, and those of more than £1.5 million which could gain access to the London stock exchange. A similar gap has existed for a long time in the international field, between short-term finance through bills of exchange, used to finance commodity trade, and long-term bonds for capital formation. The gap was the difficulty in financing heavy equipment – machine tools, machinery, airplanes and the like. In the 1930s, this case of market failure was filled by government bodies such as the Export-Import Bank, the Export Credit Guarantees Department, COFACE in France, and, after the war, the Kreditanstalt für Wiederaufbau in Germany.

More recently term loans which grew up for intermediate finance in domestic banking have spread to international finance, and given the world some excitement in the debt crisis caused by excessive extension of syndicated bank loans beginning about 1971. The details of this surge and ebbing in capital flows are too fresh in our minds to justify my providing a full account here of the Third World debt crisis. I would, however, note that it strikes me as exactly analogous to the foreign-lending episodes from London in 1825, 1857, 1866 and 1890, not to mention 1873 in Central Europe, with a displacement, followed by new profit opportunities, euphoria, overshooting, distress, and a financial crisis or not, depending upon whether or not there is a lender of last resort. From 1825 to 1913, that lender of last resort was the Bank of England, occasionally assisted by the Bank of France, the Bank of Hamburg and the State Bank of Russia. Today it is the International Monetary Fund, occasionally assisted by the Federal Reserve System and the Bank for International Settlements.

A complete taxonomy of long-term lending would include governmental provisions of various sorts, not only the trade finance for equipment just mentioned, but foreign aid under various programs, and even the intergovernmental agency loans such as those of the World Bank. The subject is too vast, and I merely wave at it with one thought of some moment. The whiter heads among you will remember that at the end of the thirties it was thought necessary to devise means of ensuring that foreign lending would be counter-cyclical. Pro-cyclical lending of the sort that the United States indulged in in the thirties was seriously destabilizing. Developed countries first stopped lending to the Third World and then stopped buying from it. Ensuring that long-term capital flowed in an anti-cyclical pattern was recommended by a League of Nations study, and if my memory serves, by that eminent Cantabrigian, Joan Robinson, among others. But how? Governments can restrain private capital to some degree, but cannot stimulate it when it is shy. The articles of the World Bank incorporated a provision calling for it to "conduct its operations with due regard to the effects of international investment on business conditions." At an early stage the Bank begged off, saying that it was unable to carry out the mandate – presumably because of decision and execution lags – and a dominating commitment to economic growth (International Bank for Reconstruction and Development, 1949).

International financial intermediation

Adjustment in the balance of payments for capital flows through new issues ideally follows the absorption model, with an excess of savings in the lending country, and of investment in the borrowing, together creating an export surplus in the former, a deficit in the latter. (This assumes a fixed exchange rate and no borrowing to increase the money supply.) When the movement goes through trade in outstanding securities – the portfolio model – it is not clear how the balance of payments adjusts. One possibility is the absorption model: A, the lender, buys securities in B with new savings, and the B sellers use the proceeds to undertake new investment. One could possibly envisage the price-specie-flow mechanism, or an elasticities model with A's exchange rate depreciating. Perhaps the most likely outcome, however, is that investors in A have excess liquidity, while sellers in B are interested in becoming more liquid, and B's central bank holds the newly acquired foreign exchange with its domestic money counterpart. The current account remains unchanged, despite what the monetary model of the balance of payments holds. This is international financial intermediation, A investing long and borrowing short, B disinvesting long in exchange for cash. The equilibrium position becomes

$$X - M - LTC_{port} - STC_{liq} = O = G \tag{7}$$

where LTC_{port} is an outflow of portfolio capital and STC_{liq} an inflow in A, the opposite taking place in B. In effect A has provided B with liquidity. STC_{liq} belongs on the left-hand side of the equation because it is wanted in B to hold, and A is prepared to part with it. The case is identical to that presented by Jeffery Williamson (1964) when the United States borrowed to obtain money, though in that instance the money was sought for transactions, not holding. But liquidity adds to welfare. It is an appropriate item of trade.

I should add that Walter Salant has shown that direct foreign investment can also be used as a means of trading in liquidity. The demonstration was called for as an answer to the French complaint that the dollar system permitted the United States to buy up

French factories with money supplied by the French. Salant's contention was that liquidity preference was so strong in France, and weak in the United States, that Americans and French voluntarily swapped real assets for money (1966). There was no element of compulsion in the system.

There are two further related topics for which I must make room: first, the response of long-term capital to flexible exchange rates since 1973, and second, the present position in which the United States is sucking savings from all over the world, driving up the dollar, running a large balance-of-payments deficit on current account, and shifting, insofar as the matter can be judged from the uncertain statistics of the value of foreign investment, from a creditor to a debtor nation.

My predilection has always been for fixed exchange rates, international money if you like, based on the Hicks' theorem that two goods (monies) with a fixed price can be regarded as one. I had thought, along with the flexible-exchange-rate enthusiasts, that exchange risk under flexible rates would dry up international capital flows. It was evident that the flexible rate between the Canadian dollar and the U.S. dollar had not done so, but this was regarded as an exception. In the long run, a dollar is a dollar is a dollar, as Gertrude Stein might have said, and fluctuations presumably took place around a long-run benchmark of 1 for 1. When other countries borrowed in New York after the repeal of the Interest Equalization Tax, or borrowed in the Euro-dollar bond market, they were deliberately going short of the dollar, a speculative position, justified by the expectation that the United States was likely to inflate at a higher rate than other financially developed countries. Or so both fixed- and flexible-rate adherents thought.

This proved not to be the case. Canada was not an exception and positions in dollars were opened on both long and short sides. The matter is a puzzle. I have conjectured that in money questions, as often for goods, quantity is more important than price (1981, chap. 18). Large firms seem to borrow long-term and lend the proceeds back to the Euro-currency market on a short basis, paying the spread in the term structure of interest rates and speculating on future interest rates, in order to have certain access to money when it is needed. This is a purchase of liquidity. It may be that exchange losses which may be met through rate changes under flexibility through long-term borrowings or lendings are notionally amortized over a long period of time. Certainly it is mind-boggling to see the free and easy way that capital moves from currency to currency today with flexible rates. The rise of the dollar in 1985 to the highest level since 1971 was caused by and failed to cut off the huge inflow of capital from Europe and Japan to the United States that financed the record current-account deficits.

I have already indicated some hesitation in deciding how much to ascribe the U.S. current-account deficit to overvaluation of the exchange rate – an elasticities model – and how much to the U.S. government budget deficit that has crowded out exports and produced the current-account deficit in an absorption model. (The monetary approach to the balance of payments fits badly; firms, banks, governmental agencies, and for all I know households, are borrowing abroad, suggesting a shortage of money in the U.S. relative to other countries, whereas the import surplus on current account suggests too much money relative to demand.) Part of the inflow may represent capital flight, a sort of malaise in Europe compounded of economic discouragement and political fatalism that makes investors seek earnings and refuge in the United States. It seems to me unlikely that we have here a transfer problem, with the deficit developing to accommodate an autonomous inflow. Rather I share the general view in the United States that the U.S. governmental deficit keeps the real interest rate higher than those in Europe and Japan – where economic locomotives rest idly on sidings – attracting capital seeking higher returns and prepared to ignore exchange risk.

To the student of these matters in the 1930s it is a bizarre world. Capital flows the wrong way, from the less to the more rich, and is consumed when it arrives rather than invested in productive projects.

Development stages

Let me conclude this chapter on long-term capital by suggesting that the pattern in which capital flows from rapidly growing Japan to the slowing-down United States may not in reality be bizarre – an arbitrary outcome of a series of accidental structural changes in the two countries touched on earlier – but one that arises normally out of the stages of economic development that the two countries have reached.

Beginning with Bullock, Williams and Tucker (1919), economists have detected stages in the balance of payments of a country in the course of its development, starting with a young debtor that is going into debt, moving on to mature debtor when it begins to pay back its debt and accumulate wealth of its own, passing to young creditor when assets exceed liabilities and it accumulates net claims on the rest of the world, and ending as a mature creditor that lives off the interest and dividends on its net claims and may even consume some of its capital. While the balance of indebtedness cannot be measured precisely – one does not know for general purposes whether one ought to use book values, cost, the capitalized value of the income, or market, and if market whether quoted values or the prices at which securities and real assets could be liquidated under time pressure – and while the pattern is far from regular – the United States went through several stages in a rush in World War I, and Canada on the other hand keeps emerging from young to mature debtor and slipping back again – the stages make some sort of sense as "ideal types" and may be relevant to the Japan-United States position today. The taxonomy based on four stages collapses to two if just the balance of indebtedness is counted, or three if attention is focussed on the balance of payments on current account, reflecting the flow of capital. Or if one takes account of both the balance sheet – the balance of indebtedness, and flows – the current account – simultaneously, and notes the changes, the scheme can produce six stages, as shown in Table 1.

In his posthumously published article, Keynes suggested that the United States was about to change from being a young creditor, continuing to accumulate claims on the rest of the world, to a mature creditor that would begin to consume its wealth (1946). The forecast was premature by about a generation. Newspaper accounts in the United States observed in 1985 that the country had passed through from adult creditor to mature creditor, though the estimates, as just noted, are far from precise.

Table 1. *Balance of indebtedness and current account by development stages*

Development stage	Balance of indebtedness	Current account	Active/ passive
young debtor		passive	passive
adult debtor	debtor	balanced	
mature debtor		active	
young creditor		active	active
active creditor	creditor	balanced	
mature creditor		passive	passive

See Kindleberger, 1968, pp. 417ff.

But it is unlikely that anyone could have predicted the rise of Japan as a capital-exporting nation in 1946, or even as late as 1965.

A recent paper suggests that the capital exports to the United States from Japan were not the consequence of random arbitrary features in the structures of the two countries affecting savings – the government deficit in the United States produced by the idiosyncratic economic theories of President Reagan calling for increases in military expenditures and cuts in personal and corporate taxation, plus the eagerness of the postwar generation to borrow and live well and to spend all income other than that committed to contractual savings in pension plans and mortgage payments – plus in Japan the lack of social security, the thirteen-month payment of salaries, with that of the extra month more readily saved, and the demographic surge of births after the war, producing a generation that has to provide for its own rapidly lengthening old age. It was rather, in their view, the natural and normal consequences of "developmental stages," Japan entering the stage of young creditor at a time when the United States was moving along the S- or Gompertz curve of growth to that of mature creditor (Akiyama and Onitsuka, 1985). Europe is hard to fit into the analysis, except perhaps for Germany which like Japan discovered the fountain of national economic youth in defeat in war that destroyed all distributional coalitions that block improvements in productivity and accelerate inflation in countries that escaped that purging fire (Olson, 1982). Britain and France to a lesser extent are a few years ahead of the United States in economic maturity, and have consumed a great deal of their foreign wealth already. To the extent that they invest in the United States rather than at home, it must be for quite other reasons than the development stages, such as economic pessimism about the future of Europe.

The structural and the developmental stages of the higher rates of saving in Japan and Germany than in the United States are not entirely contradictory but to some extent fit together (Norton, 1986). To the extent they do not, it is probably impossible to determine econometrically which dominates the capital flow. My intuition tells me, however, that the task of eliminating the governmental deficit and stimulating personal savings in the United States is a formidable one, not readily responsive to readily achieved changes in policy. Similarly while Japanese savings may decline as the immediate postwar generation gets older, the process of reducing personal and corporate savings in Japan will meet forces that are deeply resistant. If so, the flow of long-term capital to the United States from the Pacific area will not be readily reversed.

At the Kemp-Bradley "Summit" in November 1985 on flexible exchange rates and the possibility of achieving greater stability, one discussant viewed it as obscene to have the Japanese people, living in a severe shortage of housing space, sending their savings to the United States to be invested in hotels and offices destined to remain underoccupied. It is hard to quarrel with that judgement.

3   Short-term capital

The 1937 view

In my dissertation of fifty years ago, the principal finding was that equilibrium in the balance of payments of a country meant that movements of gold and short-term capital should be nil on balance. The proposition was put forward in prose, rather than with the identities used in these lectures that resemble algebra. What I in effect came out with was

$$X - M - LTC = O = STC + G \tag{4b}$$

that we have already encountered in the first chapter as basic balance. My supervisor, the late Professor James W. Angell, did not agree. He argued persistently for gold movements as the measure of disequilibrium, or in today's notation

$$X - M - LTC - STC = O = G \tag{4c}$$

a variation on (2) p. 4, with LTC and STC brought back into the balance. I was grateful to him at the time, and remain so, for having the tolerance to allow me to disagree with his older, and at least presumptively wiser view. And the burden of this chapter is that despite the fierce belief in one's own ideas in youth, over time, and along with much of the world, I have backed away – or perhaps pushed forward – from this position.

First let me note that equilibrium in (4b) has to be qualified in a number of respects – for inventories, for the relations between gold flows and short-term capital flows, one aspect of which can be subsumed under the heading of Gresham's Law, and third, for positions in the forward-exchange market.

Inventories

Firstly, observe that the analysis assumes that exports are out of current production and imports go into absorption. There are no large offsetting changes in inventories. To limit ourselves to one of four possible variations, if imports are stockpiled, rather than consumed or invested, the true relationships in the balance of payments are distorted. Imports in effect are borrowed from the future. In 1936 and 1937, the world was misled in thinking the U.S. current account was in balance as M approached X. The fact was that businesses were stockpiling raw materials against inflation in fear of John L. Lewis, the labor leader. When inventory accumulation was reversed, imports fell precipitously revealing that the current account had been in surplus all along. In the same fashion, the German deficit in 1950 at the time of Korea was overstated by stockpiling, and the British deficit hidden by unduly low imports and a running down of inventory that later had to be replaced. If one likes, one can think of changes in inventories as belonging with short-term capital and gold on the right-hand side of the equation. Increases in inventories are close to increases in reserves, and decreases like reserve losses.

Gresham's Law

Secondly, it is not enough under the gold-exchange standard for $STC + G$ to be O. In addition to cancelling, they must both be absolutely small. In my dissertation of 1937, I argued that short-term capital can complement gold or substitute for gold. Assume that short-term capital is embodied in deposits, rather than bills of exchange. Gold and deposits are both international money. They may be added to one another in performing money's functions. Or a Gresham's Law problem may crop up, with money-holders switching out of gold into foreign exchange, as at the time of the 1936–7 "golden avalanche," or out of foreign exchange into gold – the central banks of the gold bloc converting $750 millions in dollar deposits into gold from September 1931, when sterling went off gold, until the end of the year. Even if the movements in gold and foreign exchange are of opposite sign and cancel out, large movements in opposite directions signal financial crisis that may lead to breakdown.

Largely with an eye to the provision of the right amount of the liquidity in the system, Robert Triffin criticized the gold-exchange standard as an absurdity (1958). That seemed to me misguided. As I shall detail later, under optimal circumstances international financial intermediation can smoothly, cheaply and efficiently provide the international monetary system with the amount of liquidity needed. The problem with the gold-exchange standard was not its provision of the wrong amount of liquidity, but its instability. With two monies, there is a risk of convulsive switching from one to the other. In these circumstances, the market approximates less closely a balance than a see-saw. Gresham's Law was originally applied – not by Gresham to be sure, though he got the credit – to the problem posed by a fixed mint ratio between the prices of gold and silver, and a variable market ratio. Bimetallist proponents held that the mint price would stabilize the market price. In practice, the market price often dominated the mint price, revealing that the mint ratio was out of line and setting up dumping of the overvalued money and hoarding of the undervalued. The law is not limited to bimetallism, but is more general, applying to two metals, to metal and paper money, to two monies, deposits and currency – any two assets in fact that have a customary price relationship between them. I harbor a Gresham-Law-like concern over the French recent practice of taking her surpluses in gold and paying for deficits by borrowing dollars in the Euro-currency market through parastatal corporations such as *Electricité de France*, leaving her long of gold and short of dollars. Even with future payments balanced on some reasonable basis, there is a Gresham's Law danger here if the price of gold becomes more volatile.

Positions in the forward-exchange market

Thirdly, one should make allowance in equation (4b) for any substantial central-bank position in forward exchange that disguises a spot position. Forward contracts go into balance sheets only as a footnote, and of course as affecting both assets and liabilities of the future. But changes in the forward position of a country with the outside world, like changes in inventories of foreign-trade goods, disguise what is actually taking place, or what has taken place. In 1927 and 1928, the Bank of France, under the governorship of Emile Moreau, hid the Bank's claim on London by swapping spot sterling forward with the private French market (League of Nations, 1944, p. 36). The sterling appeared to be owned privately, when it was in fact being held for the monetary authority. In 1967, the Bank of England hid its ultimate deficit by selling dollars to the market forward rather than spot. These forward sales represented a disguised claim on British reserves. A number of economists had taken the position, including a hint from Keynes in the *Tract on Monetary Reform*, that monetary authorities really had no need of reserves: they could sell foreign exchange forward indefinitely, rolling over old contracts as they matured and cover current deficits by selling more (1924). This view came in for a rude awakening in 1967 when the exchange market thought it likely that the Bank of England's forward contracts exceeded its reserves. At this point the market became unwilling to continue extending old contracts, and demanded delivery of dollars as contracts matured.

With the obstinacy of age I should like to recur here to the position taken on forward exchange in my dissertation, a position to which I have clung while the literature goes off in different directions. That position is that markets for forward exchange are either joined to spot markets by arbitrage, or they are not. When they are joined, they tell us nothing that we cannot deduce from the spot rate and relative interest rates in the two markets. Two markets joined are one market, and in one market there is only one price. The forward rate moves to the interest-rate parity and stays there. It can serve neither as an exact estimate of the future rate, as many economists have thought, nor as an unbiased estimator of the future rate, the position that econometricians moved to for a time when their attempts to demonstrate the former proved illusory. Moreover, when the forward rate with arbitrage moves to the interest differential the forward market adds little to the capacity for hedging positions; large firms with access to credit in both markets can hedge by borrowing in one market, and investing the spot proceeds in short-term instruments in the other. The issue is merely one of whether it is cheaper to hedge in the spot or forward market as a question of transactions costs, and for large firms, the costs are often cheaper in the spot market.

If the spot and forward markets are not joined because say arbitrage is forbidden – though something approximating arbitrage is almost certain to take place through exporters and importers shifting back and forth between spot and forward markets as it pays them – akin to the leads and lags through changing payment terms in trade when short-term capital movements are forbidden – then the forward market has to clear itself and may reflect traders' and speculators' views of the future spot rate, possibly accurately, but at least in unbiased fashion. In this circumstance, the forward market tends to be thin, erratic, and relatively useless for hedging which is still possible, absent exchange controls, via the spot market and borrowing/lending. Paul Einzig criticized this early position of mine on the ground that it was "static," whereas his view was "dynamic" (1937), words that convey no clear meaning to me in this context. I hypothesize that he meant that arbitrage between the two markets was somewhere between perfect and zero, so that the two outcomes in the polar outcomes are irrelevant. But until one has some idea whether the arbitrage is nearer perfection or zero, and stable in amount or changing, it is hard to say anything much at all about the forward-exchange market.

The old taxonomy

Let us, however, set aside these qualifications and diversions and return to taxonomy. In my 1937 effort I divided short-term capital movements into "autonomous," moved by such considerations as flight from confiscatory taxation; "compensating," i.e., responding directly to changes in other items in the balance of payments as trade credits did or the counterpart of long-term borrowing; "induced" that responded to changes in interest rates; and "speculative," reacting to current or prospective changes in exchange rates.

Liquidity and official balances

While I am disinclined to dismiss that earlier classification scheme altogether, discussion after the war has proceeded on other lines, motivated partly by Triffin-like fears (1958) that evoked in Walther Lederer, then of the U.S. Department of Commerce, and later of the Treasury Staff, the "liquidity definition" of balance-of-payments equilibrium:

$$X - M - LTC - STC_{us} = O = STC_f \qquad (8)$$

(I drop gold.) STC_{us} is short-term capital belonging to United States firms and households, and STC_f represents foreign short-term claims on the United States. Lederer's argument was that American short-term claims on abroad were largely tied up in trade credits, unavailable to meet potential withdrawals of dollar deposits, represented by STC_f. One ought therefore, in his opinion, to achieve real transfer of U.S. short-term credits along with that of long-term capital flows as called for by basic balance. This definition of equilibrium was hotly debated, deemed unsatisfactory by many, and re-examined by a special committee appointed to review the question (Review Committee, 1965). The committee proposed a new definition of equilibrium, called "official balance," based on dividing short-term capital into private and official components, STC_p and STC_o, respectively. Equilibrium then became:

$$X - M - LTC - STC_p = O = STC_o \qquad (9)$$

Whereas the liquidity definition assumed that U.S. claims on the world could not be mobilized, and foreigners were liable at any instant to call on the United States to pay off their claims on the U.S., the official definition assumed that all private owners of short-term capital, American or foreign, held their claims voluntarily, whereas foreign authorities held their dollars only under sufferance, and that increases in these dollars, at least, represented a deficit.

The U.S. as a bank

The official definition had several technical deficiencies, such as the difficulty of distinguishing the ultimate owner of foreign balances when central banks undertook forward/spot dollar swaps in their own markets as a means of open-market operations. The major objection to it, however, was the thought that foreign central banks holding dollars had no use for them. It was then that Emile Despres, Walter Salant and I wrote "The Dollar and World Liquidity: A Minority View," published in the *Economist* in February 1966 when Fred Hirsch was the financial editor. (Despres *et al.*, 1966 reprinted by Kindleberger, 1981, chap. xi.) In our judgement, none of these definitions of equilibrium, or those put forward by Bergsten, Lary and others (Kindleberger, 1969 (1981)) was very helpful to understanding what was taking place. We suggested that on a reasonable view the United States had not been in disequilibrium during the 1950s and the first half of the 1960s. It had been engaged in international financial intermediation, lending long and borrowing short, providing liquidity to the world. Foreign balances were accumulated in dollars not because the United States had a current-account deficit, but because the country made loans abroad, and provided aid, together in excess of its current-account surplus. The United States was, in effect, acting as a bank to the world. The deposits of successful banks rise year after year, as did those of the United States. Other countries were like firms: an increase in foreign claims on them, net, reflected a deficit. Banks and firms differ in their vulnerability to quick liabilities, the appropriate magnitude of their reserve ratios (for firms, quick-asset ratio), and the appropriateness of lending long and borrowing short. For firms, and for countries other than the United States, basic balance was the appropriate definition of equilibrium (equation 4b). The asymmetry between the equilibrium definition for the United States and that applicable to others is exactly parallel to that under the gold standard for gold producers, and countries buying gold to add to their reserves. In the first instance gold was an export. To the importer it was money in quite a different category in the balance of payments.

Our 1966 article was regarded as of interest, but not persuasive. We perhaps failed to take account of wild-cat banking when banks kept on creating deposits by lending without building reserves and capital concomitantly. The United States finally agreed in 1966 to the creation of Special Drawing Rights (the S.D.R), put forward by some economists because of an alleged world need for liquidity, because the United States as a bank needed a means of adding to its reserves when gold was going into hoarding. Reserves for others could be created by international financial intermediation, borrowing long and lending short. The United States alone could not create reserves in this way. Milton Gilbert, Peter Oppenheimer, and a few others wanted to increase world liquidity by raising the price of gold, a practice recommended, if my memory serves, by Hayek in the 1930s. Most thought then, however, that continuous changes in the price of gold would destroy the gold mystique even faster than it ultimately disappeared – no, those words are too strong because the atavistic, not to say Freudian, instinct remains potent in many quarters.

The breakdown of Bretton Woods

If one rejects basic balance as the equilibrium criterion for the United States, the liquidity balance, and the balance of official transactions, what is left? Judging the soundness of a bank is not, in my view, a matter of precise balances or ratios, as recent discussion of bank failures in the United States amply demonstrates. In bank failures, discussion turns around an acronym CAMEL, where C stands for capital, A for asset quality, M for management, E for earnings, and L for liquidity (Flannery and Guttentag, 1980, p. 172). I should have thought that the United States had a satisfactory performance up to the Vietnam war on all but liquidity. But however adequate for a commercial bank, CAMEL is not enough for a world financial center. Satisfactory performance requires not only liquidity keeping pace in some ratio with foreign short-term liabilities, but also resistance to inflation. Perhaps this should be included under M for management. In this respect the U.S. performance from about 1964 to 1979 was lamentable. The world went short of dollars in speculative positions, with the safety of what is known as the one-way option. In 1968 the United States broke up the London gold pool that it had been mainly supplying, replacing it with the two-tier system. In 1971 came the refusal to pay gold at all (Gowa, 1983), and in 1973, flexible exchange rates. Depreciation of the dollar gave a push to inflation in the United States.

Successful short speculation against the dollar takes us back to the 1937 taxonomy and to speculative capital movements. Speculation in foreign exchange – an open or an exposed position – is to have a non-zero balance of net claims or liabilities in foreign exchange. One can debate what to count as a foreign-exchange asset or liability apart from cash, receivables and quick liabilities fixed in foreign currency. I choose to exclude inventories, plant and equipment, and to overlook most long-term assets and debts. If we put the technical issues aside, there are two reasons to maintain open exposure: one, because one thinks the foreign-exchange rate is going to change, and wants to benefit, and another, because one thinks it is not going to change, and hence that it is appropriate to ignore the risk of change altogether. In the case of long-term bonds, as noticed in the first lecture, markets seem to think, contrary to what most of us anticipated, that the net change in the exchange rate over a long period is dominated by substantial differences in interest rates. Long-term capital movements by and large have ignored foreign-exchange risk. Short-term capital more often embraces it.

A problem for monetary authorities trying to stabilize a currency after World War II was posed by the enormous increase in the volume of foreign-exchange transactions. Various centers all had increased liquidity. Multinational corporations, including banks, operated more widely in the world, readier to move money over longer distances. In addition to growth in real G.N.P., inflation increased nominal amounts of mobile capital. The horizons of money-market participants had been extended by the improvement in transport and communications, enabling them to contemplate a wider set of alternative employments for money. A heavy drain on a major financial center before World War II was $100 million a day. At the peak of financial crises in 1964, 1967,

1971, 1979 and the like, an adverse run could bring down central bank reserves by several billions of dollars in a single trading session.

The Euro-currency market

Beyond the increased liquidity of single financial centers, world liquidity was raised further in the 1960s and 1970s by the development of the Euro-currency market, trading in Europe originally but later in such centers as Bahrein and Singapore, of currencies, particularly dollars, in countries other than that in which the currency was issued. The market developed slowly because of a slip: Regulation Q in the United States limiting interest paid on time deposits did not apply to deposits by foreigners. Dollars deposited in the London branch of a U.S. bank and redeposited in New York escaped the limit. There were other advantages to dealing in Euro-currencies, escaping reserve requirements, fees for insurance, and possible surveillance or intervention by national authorities (of interest especially to Russian holders of dollars), and bringing U.S. banks through their European branches into the same time zone as the major European banks. The Euro-currency market formed an integrating interconnection around major financial centers, thickening the bilateral connections that existed among pairs.

On the foundation of the 1960s, moreover, was built an enormous mistake in monetary policy, reducing interest rated in the United States at a time when the German authorities were seeking to tighten them. Funds poured out of the United States to the Euro-dollar market in say London, where they were attracted to Germany, where the authorities were forced to mop them up and chose to redeposit them in the Euro-dollar market. The basis was established not only for term lending to Latin America through syndicated bank loans, but also for foreign-exchange speculation on an increased scale. Inexperienced banks found themselves making substantial losses from foreign-exchange speculation. In 1974 both the Herstatt Bank of Cologne and the Franklin National Bank of New York were closed by the authorities. Both guessed wrong on the direction of exchange-rate movements under floating. Herstatt's exposure was one-tenth of that of the Franklin National, a speculative bank with a bad record in lending to risky businesses in New York, going to London to borrow money for lack of a solid deposit base on its home ground, and speculating in foreign exchange with an exposure that at one time reached $2 billion (Spero, 1980, p. 113).

Speculation again

Speculation can be stabilizing or destabilizing, depending upon whether the speculators have inelastic or elastic expectations. With inelastic expectations, thinking the rate will return to its old level, speculators buy as prices fall, sell when they rise. With elastic expectations, on the other hand, a change in price is thought to signal an extended movement in the given direction, and speculators buy as the price of foreign exchange rises, sell on a falling one. As noted in Chapter 2, Milton Friedman denies the possibility of destabilizing speculation on the Darwinian ground that if speculators were to buy high and sell low they would lose money and be driven from business. But the conventional theory refers not to all speculators, but to professionals, who drive the rate up and sell out at the top, or drive it down and cover their short sales at the bottom. The persons to whom they sell at the top or from whom they buy at the bottom do lose money. These may be uninformed and laggard speculators. They are often central banks, trying unsuccessfully to stabilize the rate.

Central banks cannot afford to go bankrupt, of course, since their liabilities are used as money or high-powered money owned by the domestic banking system. If they hold foreign-exchange reserves that have declined in price – dollars, for example, bought at 4 Dm to the dollar that have declined to 2.5 Dm to the dollar, they would be bankrupt if they were an ordinary bank forced by examiners to "mark to market," but central banks are not ordinary banks. They either unconcernedly carry the foreign exchange on their books at cost, rather than market, or charge the loss to the government which issues them a special claim that becomes another central-bank asset. No. "Unconcernedly" is too strong. Central bankers dislike such losses intensely which is why in a run on a currency they will convert dollars or sterling into gold. But they should be less concerned. The danger of a long-run national loss should be less of a worry than the danger of a foreign-exchange crisis from participating with the speculators in a run, rather than helping stabilize the system by leaning against the wind.

There are cases on record, however, of professional speculators losing heavily. In 1924 the Bank of France, with the help of a $100 million loan from J. P. Morgan and Company, applied a squeeze to foreign-exchange speculators, driving the rate for the franc up from 123 to the pound on March 8 (140 in the forward three-month market) to a high of 68 in May, inducing heavy losses and even failures in banks in the Netherlands, Germany and Austria (Debeir, 1978). It is not altogether clear what definitions of stabilizing and destabilizing Friedman and others are using when they deny the possibility of destabilizing speculation. On conventional definitions, using proximate price behavior, the tracking or wide swings of rates, or movements away from purchasing-power parity, it is hard to see the justification for the position.

The psychological theory of the foreign exchanges

During the turbulent 1920s, a French economist, Albert Aftalion, propounded a psychological theory of the foreign exchanges. This held that exchange rates were dominated by sentiment, whether money markets approved of macro-economic policies or not. On bad news the franc would fall; on good news rise. The monetary authorities were helpless under the circumstances of the period from 1923 to 1926 because French government debt was largely in six-month maturities. A large amount of debt came due each week and had to be rolled over or paid off. Attempts to lock holders into long maturities all failed. If it chose, the money market could force the Bank of France to monetize a sizeable sum any week, insisting on cash for maturing Treasury bills which would equip the market with francs that could be used to buy foreign exchange. Buoyant exports and a declining government-budget deficit were of little account compared with the market's response to political events.

The psychological theory of foreign exchange was rather disdained outside of France at the time and in subsequent analysis but appears to be making a comeback, based on the strength of the dollar from 1980 down to February 1985 or to September 1985 in the face of adverse fundamentals. In his book, *The Arena of International Finance*, Charles Coombs, the late foreign-exchange trader for the Federal Reserve Bank of New York and the U.S. Treasury Stabilization Fund, asserted twice (1976, pp. 116, 235) that foreign-exchange traders can lose their shirts betting on long-run fundamentals, as opposed to "market forces" – read psychological factors. Most economists think the dollar was seriously overvalued – by perhaps 30 or even 40 percent – in the first three quarters of 1985 when the United States has a deficit on current account of $130 billion in 1985 and higher numbers in sight. Professional forecasters have been advising their clients since 1982 that the dollar was too high and headed for a fall. But it kept climbing, reaching a peak in February 1985. Since then it has been brought down a considerable distance, especially against the yen where the bilateral deficit of the United States was at its most acute. In part the decline was a belated response to fundamentals as opposed to the psychological theory of foreign exchange that led some observers to predict that the dollar would stay strong, and even gain, so long as President Reagan was in the White House and Paul Volcker in the chairmanship of the Federal Reserve Fund.

In the spring of 1985, however, a change took place that produced a psychological impact in the opposite direction. When James Baker and Donald Regan changed places in the Reagan administration, Baker leaving the White House staff for the secretaryship of the Treasury and Regan the Treasury for the White House, a change in government attitude toward the dollar and international finance was produced. Regan, possibly influenced by the monetarist economist, Beryl Sprinkel, had been a strong advocate of accepting whatever exchange rate the market chose to fix. In the spring of 1985, indeed, when European central banks and the Bank of Japan tried to bring the dollar down by selling off dollar reserves for home currencies, the Federal Reserve Bank of New York, which does not operate in foreign exchange except on instruction from the Treasury, sold dollars for foreign currencies in what was evidently a half-hearted fashion, convincing the speculators that the movement would fail. When Regan later left the Treasury, Sprinkel shifted to the chairmanship of the Council of Economic Advisers, a post without operational responsibilities. In September 1985, Secretary Baker called a meeting of the five leading finance ministers – the Federal Republic of Germany, France, Japan, the United Kingdom and the United States – at the Hotel Plaza in New York, where agreement was reached to bring the dollar down. Further initiatives were taken to urge commercial banks to renew maturing loans to Third World countries and to lend new monies, and, in 1986, the decision to coordinate the reduction of interest rates in the several world financial markets so as to stimulate production throughout the industrial world without giving rise to short-term capital flows. It is too early to reach a firm conclusion whether the Reagan administration has changed its view on international monetary policy, flexible exchange rates and cooperation, though the president has ordered Secretary Baker (doubtless on the initiative of Baker himself) to study these issues and report in the fall of 1986.

Liabilities to foreigners and the money supply

This discussion of short-term capital is perhaps spotty, but there are a number of topics worth pursuing if only as a recital of fiercely debated issues and an agendum for research. One question is whether foreign deposits should be counted as part of the money supply. In the 1930s in the United States they were not. Today they are. I hope I may be forgiven if I lack the inclination to pinpoint exactly when the definitional change was made. A case can be made for inclusion or exclusion. Foreign balances turn over against exports and imports, i.e., goods and services, and are used in making and unmaking domestic investments by foreigners. One basis for exclusion, on the other hand, is that they are more like near money, held largely for liquidity, as reserves, especially the balances belonging to foreign central banks. But one can also think in terms of the alternative uses of domestic and foreign-owned deposits. Foreigners who hold dollars as a short-term speculation presumably have different alternative uses, i.e., different opportunity costs, than domestic holders.

The issue arose in the discussion of the German inflation of 1923. Holtfrerich observed that a significant element in the course of the inflation had been the shifts in foreign, largely American expectations. When the mark originally fell after having been freed from controls in 1919, Americans, often of German origin, bought marks and mark balances, anticipating an eventual return of the rate to par. Americans made investments in land, government securities, equities, but especially in currency and deposits. Holtfrerich noted that as much as 45 percent of the German money supply was in foreign hands, and that the Reichsbank had to issue more domestic money to maintain domestic business (1982). Debeir, a Frenchman, argued that there should be no distinction between American and German holdings of marks. Both groups had access to the same information, and both were in position to speculate for or against the mark (1982). In 1924–6 when there was speculation against the French franc, it was true that there was foreign speculation, but most of the money moved abroad was French. The issue is one about which it is difficult to be dogmatic. In the German case, Americans holding marks and Germans holding marks had different alternative uses for them: if he bought goods, the American was likely to buy American goods, whereas the German was likely to buy German goods. American mark holdings had a different velocity than German, or belonged more completely to the liquidity circulation (to use Keynes' distinction from the *Treatise on Money* (1930)), whereas German balances were more fully in the transactions circulation. In the case of French balances in England after the Poincaré stabilization of 1926, there was no serious likelihood that they would remain in Britain and constitute part of the regular British money supply. Their normal "habitat," as some monetary theorists use the concept, was France. The question was not whether the balances would return to France, but when, and at what exchange rate.

In the world of today, things may have changed somewhat, at least in special circumstances. The heavy foreign borrowing by Mexico from 1979 to 1982 was partly to cover investment for growth, partly to meet a deficit on current account caused by inflationary consumption spilling over into imports. It was, however, to a great extent required to finance the export of capital to the United States. A journalist estimates that in the period 1974–85, Mexico borrowed $97 billion through syndicated bank loans and used half of it to finance $50 billion of capital flight. The estimates are highly imprecise, but run to the further effect that Argentina's capital outflow amounted to 60 percent of its foreign borrowing, Venezuela's to almost 100 percent, while for the Philippines the ratio was 25 percent and for Brazil 11 percent. In the Mexican case, roughly a quarter of its borrowing was from United States banks, but a much higher percentage of the capital flight went to that country, leaving the United States on balance a net debtor to Mexico (Henry, 1986).

This is another form of international intermediation or recycling: U.S. banks lend money to Mexico and Mexican capitalists lend money to the United States by buying dollar deposits in U.S. banks. If the flight money goes into U.S. treasury bills and notes, it is as if the U.S. banks lend to the treasury by way of Mexico City.

If the Mexican capitalists in due course repatriate the funds to their normal habitat, they will have earned substantial profits and the Mexican monetary authorities corresponding losses. At the same time the authorities will recoup sizeable amounts of dollars available to reduce their debts to foreign banks. On the other hand, with the increasing internationalization of the payments practices of the average business, many Mexican firms may decide to leave transactions balances abroad, drawing on them for foreign and domestic payments as needed. In inflationary Israel, a fair proportion of domestic transactions is conducted in dollars. The day may arrive, if it has not done so already, when business in many countries will use dollars, Deutschemarks, Swiss francs, or yen virtually anywhere, creating confusion for statisticians and monetarists over what should be counted in the national money supply.

Like Shakespeare, Samuel Johnson, Mark Twain and Adam Smith, Bagehot is full of quotations. A favorite of mine is "Men of business in England do not like the currency question. They are perplexed to define accurately what money is; *how* to count they know, but *what* to count they do not know" (1857 (1978), IX, p. 319). Bagehot of course was discussing coin, notes, deposits of various sorts – and the list could be extended today – for domestic varieties. In present circumstances, some balances in financial centers perhaps belong in the money supplies of a number of countries.

More international financial intermediation

International financial intermediation has been discussed in these lectures in many forms: large two-way movements of long-term capital, long-term capital one way and gold or short-term capital the other, Mexican borrowing abroad through syndicated bank loans and exporting capital to the lending countries in speculative flight. I should like to recur to two old-fashioned principles of lending long and borrowing short, and vice versa, and not solely for antiquarian interest. I have in mind the traditional overdraft facilities of Commonwealth governments and perhaps businesses in London, and the colonial currency boards of the dependent empire operated in sterling.

In the typical case of long-term borrowing, a government would sell bonds in London and hold the proceeds pending disbursement, thus borrowing long and lending short half the proceeds on the average over the period of payout. In some dominions, notably Australia, the timing was the contrary. Federal and state governments would finance their overseas spending through overdrafts, thus borrowing at short term, and delay selling bonds until the cumulated overdraft had reached such proportions that the London banks thought it time to pay them down. Instead of borrowing and lending back the proceeds for a time, Australia would borrow on short account and then pay off the overdraft with a long-term loan, ending up with long debt and a fresh line of overdraft credit. The system worked well until 1928 when the long-term market for foreign bonds dried up. With large overdrafts and the impossibility of borrowing long-term to reduce them, Australia had to depreciate her pound almost immediately when the trouble came in October 1929.

Colonial currency control boards right after World War II

earned a bad reputation that I think undeserved. These boards in dependent colonies such as the Gold Coast, Jamaica, Kenya, Malaysia and the like issue local monies against holdings of sterling. Many observers claimed that the poor colonies were being coerced to lend money to rich England – at least it was then regarded as rich. But the error was the same I think I detect in the monetary approach to the balance of payments. Colonial balances in London were not always accumulated through export surpluses. Foreign money can be borrowed. The colonial currency boards typically borrowed at long term in London to acquire sterling. Liquidity was obtained at the cost of the difference between the long- and the short-term rate of interest. The case of international financial intermediation vitiates the argument of those who claimed that London exploited the little black colonies, while helping their big white sisters, the dominions, as Dennis Robertson put it (1953). The same reasoning further vitiates the case that the United States earned billions of dollars of seigniorage from the dollar-exchange standard. If there had been no interest on foreign short-term dollar claims, if holders of dollars were not free to transfer them elsewhere, and if the world had not borrowed long term in New York, the accusation might have been substantial. In the event, however, the United States earned the difference between the long- and the short-term rates of interest as a payment for providing liquidity through intermediation; this payment was relatively small because the term structure of interest rates in the United States was flatter than in most countries holding dollar balances.

The colonial currency board system was not a bad one in operation. If a colony ran a deficit, it drew down its sterling holdings and was forced to cancel an equivalent sum of money at home, thus promoting balance-of-payments adjustment. Moreover, the deficit had its financing provided in advance. Netting out the intermediation and the deficit, the operation could be regarded as the ultimate inward transfer in real terms of the long-term borrowing that created the sterling balance. It was perhaps unnecessary to have domestic money vary with sterling balances pound for pound on the average. As in the organization of the Bank of England, one could have had a substantial "fiduciary issue" of domestic government securities against which there were no exchange reserves, but one-for-one foreign-exchange reserves above that. At the margin, the system was safe and efficient, quite similar to the present practice of multinational corporations borrowing long when they contemplate a big project and holding the proceeds as idle balances until the time comes to spend them for the project. When it was abandoned with independence for the colonies, troubles ensued. An analogous defense of the gold- or the dollar-exchange standard is set out in equation (7) of the second chapter, seen from the viewpoint of the short-term capital, not the long.

Foreign exchange as reserve assets – a symmetrical rule?

If exchange is used as international money, why must it be asymmetrical? As we shall see presently in discussing swaps, in crisis it need not be. For normal working, however, it must. There is a N-1 problem here. If either country can meet a bilateral imbalance, the surplus country acquiring foreign exchange or the deficit country paying it out, the system is underdetermined. Monetary authorities on the two sides may find themselves both rushing in, or both standing aside in the Gaston-Alphonse manner. Some economists have called for a rule, either that the surplus country always takes action while the deficit country is passive, or vice versa. Neither rule is supportable. If the surplus country accumulates exchange on the deficit country at each fluctuation around a long-run equilibrium position, international reserves will keep mounting, never be reduced. If the deficit country always pays out, world reserves continuously decline. The only device for maintaining world reserves about a stable trend is to have one reserve center which is passive, while others increase their reserves in periods of surplus, reduce them in deficit. According to the Mundellian rule, the reserve center should hold its price level steady, disregarding its balance of payments that is the counterpart of the balance of payments of its trading partners. If the balances of the latter add algebraically over time to zero, so will that of the center.

The swap network

Swaps are a different matter. Swaps are needed for foreign-exchange crises. They provide instant liquidity. On trend I am a monetarist, but in crisis I believe in new infusions of money. There is of course an ambiguity here, as widely in economics: how does one get back on trend after a crisis, or how to get the good genie back into the bottle when its work is done? In a world of trends and crises, however, it is a recipe for disaster to insist on an inelastic money supply, having in mind only trend, and denying the possibility of crisis. This truth was discovered many times, the hard way, and enunciated long before Walter Bagehot by such perceptive people as Henry Thornton, Sir Francis Baring and Thomas Joplin.

Swaps are of course a modern invention, having been created instantaneously in March 1961 at the time of the British exchange crisis by the so-called Basle agreement concluded among central bankers at the Bank for International Settlements. The initiative came from the United States, and in proportions between Robert V. Roosa, the Undersecretary of the Treasury, and Charles Coombs of the Federal Reserve Bank of New York that are unknown to me. Like the Euro-currency market, moreover, the development of the swap network grew like Topsy, in evolutionary fashion, rather than emerging fullblown from agreements concluded at an international conference called by leading nations to solve a particular problem. While the practice is new, the germ of the idea can be found in discussion dating back to the nineteenth century (testimony of Michel Chevalier, Ministère des Finance, *et al.*, 1867, III, p. 105, VI, p. 187) and in the interwar period during the crisis of 1931–3 (Jørgen Pedersen, League of Nations, 1934, pp. 132–3).

Swaps work, however, only among financial centers that trust one another to tidy up after the trouble has been overcome. They are available only to insiders. The doctrine of the lender of last resort is subject not only to the paradox of moral hazard – insurance weakens the incentive to guard against risk – but to the ethical dilemma that while insiders are likely to be taken care of, outsiders are frequently abandoned to an unkind fate. There was the recent trauma of the fringe banks in London in 1974, but as an amateur of economic history, I have fresh in mind the regional banks in France in 1848, the Union Générale of Lyons in 1881, the Bank of the United States in 1930, and many more.

The availability of swaps to the sophisticated financial centers is not automatic, to be sure. In 1965 France withdrew its participation in the swap line put together for the United Kingdom. Susan Strange regarded the action as a breach of the standard of central-bank freemasonry (1976, p. 61). In 1977 all central banks agreed that Britain should look to help from the International Monetary Fund first, rather than as on earlier occasions end up there to fund any swaps that had not been reversed in six months. The Third World, too, may on occasion get a bridging swap from the Federal Reserve Bank of New York while waiting for the deliberate processes of the I.M.F. to bring forth the necessary assistance.

Capital controls

The I.M.F. was not designed to cope with financial crisis. It was devised to handle current-account difficulties of a reversing or perhaps nonrecurring sort. Troubles arising from capital flows were to be dealt with by controls. As early as 1949, however, it was found that it was impossible to clamp down on short-term capital movements without controlling the credit bargains of individual transactions on current account. Short-term capital moved easily through the leads and lags, as credit terms were varied on exports and imports. Nor were controls on long-term capital effective, especially in Latin countries where the tradition of passive acquiescence to government regulations is stunted. The United States Interest Equalization Tax, Gore Amendment applying the tax to bank loans, the Voluntary Credit Restraint Program covering direct investment, and the Mandatory Control which replaced it, all imposed in the 1960s and removed in 1972, for the most part merely diverted the outflow of capital from the United States from one conduit to another. Belgian and French attempts to establish a dual exchange-rate structure, with separate markets and rates for current-account and capital transactions rarely developed rates more than three or four percent apart, as arbitrage found crevices in the structure to penetrate. In the 1930s Germany and Italy buttressed their exchange controls with the death penalty for violations, although I am unaware of any instance when it was carried out.

Capital flight takes many forms and has many stimuli. Among the stimuli are persecution, taxation regarded as confiscatory, higher possible earnings abroad than at home, and the like. But capital flight in many instances is a form of middle-class strike against the government. Labor goes on strike, with picketing, boycotts, sit-ins and other forms of expressing unwillingness to cooperate. In two cases in France after labor had achieved a favorable settlement – the Accord de Matignon won by the Front Populaire in June 1936, and the Accord de Grenelle following the *évenements de mai–juin* (events of May–June 1968, when student riots were followed by a general strike on the part of labor) – the middle class in opposition expressed its dissatisfaction by exporting capital abroad. A narrow economic reading might regard the action as a speculative position based on the prospect of currency devaluation. A broader socio-political view would call it a middle-class strike. In Italy in 1963 the identification was clearer, since there was no initial strike of labor: the Socialist government nationalized the electrical industry, and the middle class started carrying its money in packets to Switzerland to such an extent that highway robbers found it profitable to work on the main highway leading to Lugano.

The world has become discouraged with control over international capital movements as nigh to impossible to administer against the clever and the guileful. Many developing countries maintain a facade of exchange controls, though the condition of most of them is porous. The I.M.F. accordingly places reliance on macro-economic policy, and makes commitments to restraint in monetary and fiscal areas a condition of its assistance. There is naturally considerable disagreement between the Fund and countries in trouble, whether the Fund is too ideological in its insistence on contractionary policies and ambitious targets of reduced inflation, too ready to blame the borrowers in trouble when some of their loans have been pushed on them and some of their difficulties are the result of circumstances beyond their control (Williamson, 1983). In defense of the Fund, however, it may be said that while it leaned heavily on the borrowing countries it aided, it also pressed hard to require the lending countries to stretch out their terms on old loans, reduce charges, and even advance new money.

Coordinating monetary policy

After World War II, balance-of-payments adjustment among developed countries was sought through coordination of macroeconomic policy only to a limited extent. Under the gold standard from perhaps 1870 to 1913, it was deemed to be automatic. Countries gaining gold expanded; those losing gold contracted. There were occasions in the interwar period, as in 1927 on the Long Island estate of Ogden Mills, the U.S. Secretary of the Treasury, when Benjamin Strong of the New York Federal Reserve Bank, Montagu Norman of the Bank of England, Charles Rist of the Bank of France, and Hjalmar Schacht of the Reichsbank consorted to relieve the pressure on British gold and to divert French gold acquisitions from London to New York. The accomplishments of the Tripartite Monetary Agreement of 1936 were miniscule, except symbolically. After World War II, cooperation in monetary and fiscal policy was presumably advanced through monthly meetings of central-bank heads at the Bank for International Settlements at Basle, through Working Party No. 3 of the Organization for Economic Cooperation and Development in Paris, and through occasional ad hoc gatherings such as that held at Chequers in 1968 at the instigation of Henry H. Fowler, U.S. Treasury Secretary. In the late 1970s and 1980s, annual summit meetings among five to seven heads of state were initially thought of as providing an opportunity for coordination of economic policy, but developed fairly rapidly into ceremonial pageantry. The United States, possibly taking advantage of the passivity called for in a pivotal financial center under an asymmetric system conscious of the N-1 problem, shifted fairly early under President Nixon to a policy of benign neglect. In the spring of 1971, the Board of Governors of the Federal Reserve System, as already noted, pursued monetary policy in an opposite direction to that of the Bundesbank, and unleashed a flood of dollars on the world. In March 1986, on the other hand, the world made a beginning of a return to monetary coordination that may or may not be followed through as Japan, West Germany and the United States lowered discount rates in concert in the conviction that inflation was coming under control and that action was needed to encourage investment to sustain recovery. An attempt to undertake the United States action independently, led by vice-chairman Preston Martin of the Board of Governors of the Federal Reserve System ended in his defeat by Chairman Paul Volcker, a concerted reduction by the three central banks, and Mr Martin's resignation from the Board. Paul Volcker's insistence on concerted action seems to have been motivated less by devotion to coordination of money policy than to the fear that without parallel reductions abroad, there might have taken place a capital outflow from the United States with a resultant weakening of the dollar. Whether the incident will constitute a single episode like Long Island in July 1927 and Chequers in January 1968, or the start of sustained coordination, is impossible to determine at this juncture. Secretary Baker's report to President Reagan on foreign-exchange policy at the end of 1986 may recommend further steps toward coordination of monetary policies – evolutionary or large and discontinuous – or it may not.

Another failure to coordinate has been found in fiscal policy. President Carter initiated a program of locomotives (of the macro-economic sort) to pull the world out of the 1974 depression caused by the oil shock, with the United States, Europe and Japan all called upon to run budget deficits to expand output. The United States carried through while Europe and Japan held back, the United States balance of payments turned sharply deficitary, and inflation, aided by the second oil shock of 1979, picked up sharply. The Federal Reserve Board responded with a harrowing contractionary monetary policy from August 1979. The ensuing depression pushed President Carter out of office in 1980. President Reagan took over, having been seduced by the siren-song of supply-side economics. He lowered taxes, increased spending for defense, and, contrary to his expectations, enlarged the government deficit well beyond anything previously experienced in peacetime in the United States. Income spilled over into imports, confirming the central bank in its judgement of the wisdom of tight monetary policy. Inflation came down, business expansion continued, but high interest rates attracted capital from abroad which kept the dollar high and gave another elasticities fillip to the import surplus. The strong upward movement of the dollar was spurred by speculative pushes, interrupted at the end of February 1985 by a squeeze against shorts in Europe and the United States, engineered mainly by European central banks. With the beginnings of coordination of monetary policy, a similar about-face may take place in the fiscal field, where, to be sure, timing expenditure and tax measures is especially difficult.

At a meeting of the American Economic Association in Dallas in December 1985, Alexandre Lamfalussy, then Economic Adviser now Managing Director of the Bank for International Settlements, observed that the world monetary system was experiencing four revolutions at once: a regime of flexible exchange rates not regarded as temporary, new and cheaper transport and communications knitting world financial markets tightly together, a variety of new financial instruments of an innovative sort, and spreading financial deregulation (1985). The Austrian School goes so far as to advocate the abandonment of central banking and a return to free banking in which money ceases to be a public good, but becomes a private good issued by anyone who chooses to do so, in competitive markets. It takes as its model Scottish banking of the eighteenth century (White, 1984, and papers by Yeager, White, Timberlake, Hayek in Siegel, ed., 1984; papers by Timberlake *et al.*, 1985), disregarding the failure of the Ayr bank in the "speculative frenzy" of 1772 (Checkland, 1975, pp. 127ff), that spread financial crisis to London, Amsterdam and Berlin. They dismiss the example of wild-cat banking in Michigan, the unhappy results of which are ascribed to regulation (White, 1983, p. 278). Speculation under complete deregulation is anticipated to be stabilizing, short-term capital movements helpful, in the right direction and amount. Gresham's Law, if encountered at all, will work the other way, good money driving out bad as suppliers insist on receiving only the best money, rather than buyers insisting on spending only the worst.

I see no way to judge this rosy forecast of the outcome of decontrol and deregulation with any degree of certainty, but as the French say, *Je m'en doute*. My instinct and my reading of history – I have no mathematical model on the subject in which I have confidence – suggests we should head the other way: to a fixed exchange rate in the fullness of time, i.e., one world money, and to co-ordinated monetary policies, i.e., a single monetary policy for the world. I must confess I see no easy path to such an outcome, nor any likelihood of an early achievement of it, but this seems to me first best, and the target for which we should aim. I advocate attempts to stabilize long-term lending to developing countries through such institutions as the World Bank and the regional development banks, plus the world capital market though that is not subject to control, and pressure to keep trade as free as possible. We should maintain lenders of last resort both nationally and internationally, albeit cultivating enough ambiguity as to who would be saved under what circumstances so as not to unduly encourage carefree finance. The model for the world should be the integrated financial market of a single country, with one money, free movements of capital at long and short term, the quantity theory of money employed on trend, but free discounting in periods of trouble. Such a world will be full of ambiguity, paradox, uncertainty and problems. Such it seems to me is the human condition. It seems to be nonsense, however, to think it is safe to adopt a deductive theory of international finance, based on strong priors, lock the door and throw the key away, achieve financial Nirvana by casting aside the Darwinian financial lessons of a quarter of a millennium in exchange for an interesting theory.

4 Financial deregulation and integrated world capital markets

As just noted, Alexandre Lamfalussy has observed that the world monetary system is experiencing four revolutions at once: 1) flexible exchange rates not regarded as temporary; 2) new and cheaper transport and communication knitting world financial markets together; 3) a variety of new financial instruments that the world needs experience in learning to handle; and 4) rapidly spreading financial deregulation (1985). He observed the difficulty of proceeding on several different, albeit interrelated, fronts simultaneously. I was reminded of paying a visit with my brother-in-law to the barn of a neighbor where the latter was building an experimental sailing schooner of considerable size and cost. At least three major innovations were incorporated in the design and construction: a monocoque hull, like an airplane body, in which the outer skin carries the stress; lee-boards that could be independently raised or lowered, as in a Dutch sailing barge, instead of a keel or centerboard; and rigid sails each resembling half an airplane wing stood on end on the deck. My brother-in-law sagely observed that it was useful to undertake only one radical innovation at a time so that when the project failed, one could isolate where the trouble lay. I choose, however, to conclude these lectures by following Lamfalussy's four revolutions – in rather a different order – emphasizing primarily the related questions of deregulation and world integration of capital markets.

Flexible exchange rates

The revolution in the adoption of flexible exchange rates in 1973 is now, if not over, at least subsiding, and encountering a possible counter-revolutionary movement in two respects, only one of which has been discussed in earlier chapters. U.S. Secretary of the Treasury James Baker's initiative to explore greater stability of exchange rates has been referred to and applauded. What I have not dealt with is the European Monetary Agreement that represents an approach to greater exchange-rate stability on the Continent. Its success thus far has not been spectacular, since a series of mini-devaluations by various of its members has been required to keep the agreement going. It nonetheless makes progress by continuing to exist and cultivating cooperation in the formation of macro-economic policies among the participants that is building the expectation of continuing to exist in the future. The E.M.A. may well prove to have a critical importance less in its own right than as a model for world exchange-rate stability and coordination of macro-economic problems.

Before moving on from the exchange-rate revolution, however, it is useful to take note of Richard Cooper's prediction for the year 2010 of a credibly fixed set of world exchange rates, with a single world monetary authority and a single world monetary policy (1984, pp. 30ff). It is understandable that Lamfalussy should have been wary of the flexible exchange-rate system in 1984, just prior to the peak of the dollar's overvaluation, and at the height of concern for overshooting. But the beginnings of a reaction were gradually becoming visible, a reaction that grew in promise in 1985. It would take me too far from my topic to discuss the steps leading from flexible rates to greater stability – whether target zones, crawling pegs, coordinated intervention or other devices. Let me leave the matter with the good news to those of us that believe in international money that the tide seems to be turning. But I note to myself that I have been wrong before.

New financial instruments

Innovation in the fashioning of new financial instruments has been going on for at least a millennium, albeit with greater intensity since World War II. The last decades have seen the development of Euro-currencies and Euro-bonds, of the Special Drawing Right (S.D.R.) and the European Currency Unit (E.C.U.), of unit-of-account bonds, currency swaps, interest swaps, repos – a device for selling a security with a contract to buy it back later at a set price to gain short-term liquidity – a bewildering panoply of options and futures that have spread from puts and calls on shares to future contracts on government bonds, interest rates, stock-market indexes and the like, packaged loans in which mortgages, automobile installment paper and credit-card debt are grouped and participations in the total sold, Real Estate Investment Trust (R.E.I.T.s), money-market funds, junk bonds – bonds with high yields because of high debt/equity ratios in the companies involved, used to finance or resist the takeover of one company by another – the expansion of A.D.R.s (American Depository Receipts) to expedite trading abroad in American securities, etc., etc. Restrictions on U.S. bank geographical extensions have been loosened by the development of bank holding companies. With deregulation, to be discussed presently, banks have entered other fields such as investment counselling, business consulting and computer design and installation, while financial companies and even retailing firms have gone into various forms of banking including electronic transfers, issuance of credit cards, dealing in real estate. Non-bank banks that perform only one of the two main features of banking – attracting deposits and making loans – have been another device to escape regulation. New specialties are being developed and old specialized institutions are becoming less narrowly focussed. The Glass-Steagall Act of 1933 separating commercial banks and investment banking is under steady assault and widely regarded as an endangered species, though the analogous Italian equivalent of 1936 appears still to stand firm.

There is a danger in this, explored more thoroughly below in connection with deregulation, that in the early stages of an innovation, before markets have gained experience, some portion of the participants will overdo it, carrying the innovation beyond its capacity to bear the strain and leading, to use the rhetoric of Adam Smith, to "overtrading," sometimes followed by "revulsion" and "profusion." Innovations, that is, can constitute "displacement" that alters profit opportunities that on occasion will lead to excessive investment and instability. A casual reading of the financial pages in the United States in recent years discusses the difficulties of a Drysdale Corporation or a Lombard-Wall, the E.M.S. Company of Florida, and the like, and in early 1986, the instability created by fixed settlement days on stock-exchange options. But the question is more germane to the field of finance economists than to mine, and I proceed to deregulation and financial integration where similar occasional excitement is not altogether absent.

Deregulation

The winds of deregulation have been blowing strongly for some years now, both in such industries as airlines and trucking in the United States, and in the field of finance, and in the latter instance, both nationally all over the world and internationally. In 1973 two books appeared based on experience in South Korea. One was by Ronald McKinnon, calling for an end to what he called "financial repression" segmenting the money and capital markets to give advantages to preferred borrowers, notably the government, foreign traders, and large corporations, both native and multinational, and leaving other ordinary business able to obtain external funds, if at all, only hit or miss at exorbitant rates (1973). McKinnon advocated raising the level of interest rates in the favored sectors to the real rate of return on capital in the society. It was possible to view the question from the other end and think of lowering the rate of interest to the excluded groups by letting them bid in the favored segment for a single integrated pool of savings. The position can be simply illustrated with the familiar back-to-back partial-equilibrium diagram in international-trade theory before two markets are joined. With the favored market on the left, and amounts of savings running from right to left, as against left to right in the sector discriminated against, the two rates are widely different if repression keeps ordinary business out of the favored sector. On the other hand, if the two are joined by transferring some part of the excess savings at an equalized interest rate from the favored sector to that discriminated against, the going rate of interest can be equalized, raising that in the favored sector and lowering that in the other, as shown in Figure 1.

Edward Shaw's approach to inadequate finance in less developed countries based on his experience runs in terms of financial shallowness and depth (1973). Shallowness means a lack of financial intermediation, and that business has to find external finance, if at all, not in a central set of markets peopled with specialized institutions serving all kinds of needs, both of savers and of borrowers, but by directly seeking lenders who might be interested in lending to them. Raymond Goldsmith's *Financial Structure and Development* has demonstrated that the ratio of financial liabilities to national income in a country rises as the economy grows, starting in underdeveloped countries at some such ratio as 0.25 and levelling off in highly industrialized economies somewhere in the vicinity of 1.5 or 1.76 (1969). Financial deepening comes from the increasing number and size of financial intermediaries that assist savers to find the types of outlets they want in terms of liquidity and risk, and borrowers to acquire liabilities with which they are comfortable.

The McKinnon–Shaw message met an enthusiastic reception in portions of Latin America that were adopting free-market philosophies, but led to a wave of bank formation and lending that ended up in crashes in at least three countries – Argentina,

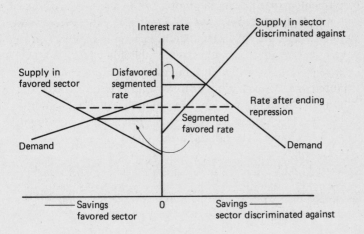

Figure 1. Financial repression when demands and supplies of savings are segmented

Uruguay and Chile (Corbo and De Melo, 1985). A posthumously published paper by Carlos F. Diaz Alejandro was entitled "Goodbye Financial Repression, Hello Financial Crash" (1985). McKinnon, once with Donald Mathieson and once alone, reviewed the experience with ending repression and concluded that it had to be done in a particular order, especially deregulating domestic capital markets before removing exchange controls to prevent capital flight (1981, 1982). Some observers have expressed the view that deregulation in banking in the United States goes too fast, and is likely to lead to troublesome excesses. The conclusion in the Latin American cases may be that the order of deregulation matters less than the speed, and that time is needed to adjust to successive steps in order to gain experience in managing the system in stable fashion.

The increase in ease and speed of transport and communication, and the reduction in cost, have made some considerable amount of deregulation almost inevitable. In the United States it is agreed that native banks must be allowed to undertake interstate banking at some orderly pace when foreign banks are permitted to establish themselves in separate states and have lately begun to do so at a rapidly rising scale. Or how can the United States and Italy maintain the separation of commercial from investment banking when domestic banks and their customers can move given transactions to London or the Netherlands Antilles where no such regulation exists? The United States government removed the 30 percent withholding (income) tax on interest paid on foreign ownership of U.S. bonds – a step widely deplored as encouraging both capital inflows to the United States and income-tax evasion – on the ground that internal communication made withholding easy to evade through tax havens and it was too difficult to undertake the effort needed to achieve compliance.

Not all financial repression or segmentation is governmentally imposed. On the contrary, much of it comes from institutional fossilization that has grown up in the private sector without planning or long-range decision. Deregulation in the London capital market, for example, involves the tearing down of the specialization that has grown up over centuries among joint-stock loans, merchant banks, acceptance houses, bill brokers, stock brokers, stock jobbers. Domestic and especially foreign banks and investment houses are acquiring firms engaged in other specialities so as to be ready to render a wider range of financial services when deregulation takes place on October 1, 1986. In the United States deregulation that permitted the development of discount brokers who offered their customers low commissions on security trading but no research or advice was one stop along the private road.

While a prominent school of thought is nervous about the extent and speed of deregulation, there is a so-called Austrian view that it should move all the way to complete withdrawal of government from all control of banking or financial activity, including the abandonment of central banking. Milton Friedman believes that the Federal Reserve System in the United States should be liquidated and replaced by a monetary control board with orders to expand the supply of high-powered money at a fixed and unalterable rate. The Austrian school goes further, and, as exemplified by F. A. Hayek in England and Roland Vaubel of the University of Mannheim in West Germany, would abolish all central monetary authority, allowing money to be issued competitively by anyone that chooses to do so. Rather than being fearful of Gresham's Law which asserts that bad money drives out good, they rely on a belief that with competition in the issue of money, good will drive out bad (1972, Vaubel, 1977). In any event, they would not fix the price of various monies issued within a nation so that they interchange at par, but anticipate that rates of exchange among domestic money issued by different bodies would vary. This would give the issuers a strong incentive, in their view, to maintain the value of their liabilities.

Three points may be raised and settled before one can readily accept this strong medicine. In the first place, while there are some cases in the historical record in which good money drove out bad, they are rare as contrasted with the opposite result. Gresham's Law is normally thought of as bad money driving good into hoarding or export. In a strong sellers' market, it may happen that a seller of a commodity in a market can insist on receiving only good money, making the law work oppositely to the usual direction. But competition among sellers is fairly usual, and choice to consumers sufficiently wide as a rule that the buyer, rather than the seller, can finally decide which money will be spent. In this circumstance, given two monies on hand, one good, one bad, the buyer will elect to spend the bad and hold the good.

Secondly, if monies of different issuers in a single jurisdiction fluctuate in value, one against the other, they cease to be money by definition, since money is the liquid asset fixed in price in terms of itself. Within countries there would have to be markets for various monies, like the foreign-exchange market for the monies of different countries, and virtually every final purchase and sale of goods would require a precedent or subsequent transaction in the market for monies.

Thirdly, the absence of all regulation of the issuance of money would place a serious burden on the ordinary unsophisticated household and small business. Federal deposit insurance in the United States, with limits set originally at $2,500 but gradually raised with inflation and increased liquidity to $100,000, was enacted in 1934 to forestall banking runs, and especially to protect the ordinary household which could not be expected to understand from analysis of balance sheets which banks were strong and which weak. Scales in butcher shops are regulated as a public good, to save the transactions cost involved in each customer checking the scale before making a purchase. In the Middle Ages, and perhaps still today for all I know, the state regulated the length of yardsticks in drapers' shops. As I write, the American press is calling attention to the need for closer security and checking of grades of leaded and unleaded gasoline, to forestall unscrupulous dealers in a few cities deceiving the normally ignorant motorist. One reason for fixed pricing in retail stores in place of bargaining – begun about the 1840s – was the rise of the department store in size beyond the point where owners could monitor their clerks to ensure that the latter did not favor relatives or friends with inordinate bargains. Another argument, urged by the Quakers, was that fixed and marked prices would enable families to send children to the store without exposing them to exploitation of their innocence. Protection of the weak would seem to be an inseparable government function, however difficult it is to draw the appropriate line.

To sum up, money as a standard of value has a public-good aspect which would be lost if each transaction required the evaluation not only of the goods to be bought and sold but also of the money to be used. It is true that Vaubel denies that money is a public good, thinking primarily, as I judge him, of the store-of-value function. He goes so far, however, as to oppose regarding the unit-of-account function in which money serves as a measuring stick as a public good that lowers transactions costs for all participants in the market (1984).

An empirical argument in favor of complete deregulation is based on the experience of the Scottish banks between 1775 and 1845 (White, 1984). Scottish "free banking" has also been extolled by Michel Chevalier, the French economist of the middle of the nineteenth century, in an argument favoring more banks to support economic expansion (1867). The White analysis begins after the failure of the Ayr bank in 1772 and stops short of that of the City of Glasgow Bank in 1878, although the latter may perhaps be blamed on the fact that free banking ended a generation earlier with the incorporation of Scottish banks into the English system. More importantly, however, it fails to emphasize that Scottish banking was in fact regulated by an informal system of note exchanges operated by the Bank of Scotland, the Royal Bank of Scotland and the British Linen Company (Checkland, 1975). These institutions would collect and hold the notes of one another and of other banks deposited by their customers, and stand ready to present an accumulation for conversion into specie whenever it was thought that the bank in question was expanding too rapidly, or taking undue risk. The practice in fact constituted a central-banking function, exercised privately. It was control. Other examples of private or semi-public banks acting to provide, however inadequately, the public good of financial stability by leaning against the wind are the Second Bank of the United States prior to Jackson's veto of its charter renewal, and the money-center banks under the National Bank of 1863 before the Federal Reserve Act (Sprague, 1910). White tends to dismiss the era of wildcat banking in the United States in the 1840s after Jackson's veto, ascribing the unhappy events of that period, especially in Michigan, to government interference rather than the absence of government regulation or the private equivalent (1983, p. 287). It requires a strong prior belief in the stability of unregulated banking to accept this view. History would appear to offer a series of persuasive demonstrations that without some regulation by government or a substitute, or with regulation that leaves open certain routes which later prove attractive, the propensity to resort to "overtrading" is endemic, especially after a change in the institutional setting.

Internationally, the pressure to deregulate becomes strong, as equity demands that banks and firms in one country should be as free to engage in profitable activities as those in another. Like small boys wanting to break away from apron strings, the first to get his mother's permission, say, to camp out overnight, leads through competitive pressure to all getting it. Deregulation may induce the discarding of safeguards that were considered important in ensuring the protection of the ordinary investor: blue-sky laws, restrictions on mail-order selling of penny stocks without a prospectus, prohibitions against insider trading and the like. The New York Stock Exchange monitors the price behavior of the stocks it quotes with computer programs designed to detect patterns of activity and prices that signal possible insider trading. It is unable to guard against the person with inside information who places an order to buy or sell a security through a public telephone call to Switzerland. I am told that this has happened so frequently that brokers in New York and London have become wary of large orders to buy or sell a given stock placed from Zurich or Geneva, and possibly resulting from the action of a Swiss institution laying off the insider order. The Swiss order may be delayed in execution for some time to see if there is breaking news that will affect the market price, up or down, which would leave a brokerage house that executed the order out of its own position holding the bag.

If it be agreed that some protection is now needed or will ultimately be needed for the unsophisticated investor and holder of money – a requirement of disclosure by the issuer of securities, such as that involved in Securities and Exchange Commission (S.E.C.) registration in the United States, or deposit insurance, and some surveillance of illicit financial dealing by insiders, drug dealers, the Mafia, plundering dictators, tax evaders, whether in foreign bank accounts or currency transactions, there should be some harmonization of various national laws, making differences in legal approaches unimportant as incentives for movement of capital. Such harmonization is difficult to achieve in a world of sovereign states. It involves ganging up on the Luxembourgs, Liechtensteins, Bahamas and the like to undermine their advantage as tax havens emanating from the sovereign right to set levels of taxation and to protect business dealing within the jurisdiction with laws ensuring secrecy. Loopholes are helpful when innocent people are being oppressed by foreign governments: the secrecy involved in Swiss bank accounts served a noble purpose in the 1930s when it protected the assets of Jews being persecuted in Nazi Germany. But the same laws that are needed in a few difficult cases are harmful when they are taken advantage of en masse to undermine the sovereignty of the countries from which the money comes, and especially when they protect the gains of criminals, scofflaws and spivs. The Swiss face an exquisite dilemma that they have tried to resolve by requiring banks to open their books when criminal activity can be proved, but not when it is only suspected. The line drawn is narrow and twisting.

Harmonization, whether in complete or in optimal deregulation, however the latter may be defined, means of course a loss of national sovereignty for the harmonizing countries. Except in the case of complete deregulation, moreover, it requires some means of agreeing on the path to be followed. In regulating security activity, and more widely in harmonizing macroeconomic policies, the question inevitably arises whether decisions are to be made hierarchically, and if so by how wide a group at the top – one country, five, seven, twenty, thirty? – and if more than one, whether by consensus or majority vote, equal weights or weighted voting with the financially more advanced countries dominating the weights. Various examples in various organizations are available: the U.N. Assembly, the I.M.F., the World Bank, E.E.C., the group of central banks invited to the monthly meeting of the Bank for International Settlements, the G-5, and so on. In the past, I have once suggested inviting representatives of the European Monetary Agreement and Japan to serve on the Federal Open Market Committee of the Federal Reserve System. This was when U.S. monetary policy dominated the Euro-dollar market and both directly and indirectly the monetary policies of much of the rest of the world. On another occasion, when the U.S. dominance had moderated, I put up the idea of conducting world monetary policy through open-market operations in various countries conducted by the B.I.S. Both notions of course are utopian, visionary, and perhaps meant to shock. More practical from a politician is the initiative of Secretary of the Treasury James Baker to stabilize world exchange rates and to lower interest rates, undertaken through the Group of Five consisting of Britain, France, the Federal Republic of Germany, Japan and the United States. It is illustrative of the difficulty of decision-making in the area that both Canada and Italy felt aggrieved at having been left out and were included after the Tokyo summit. The fact that the initiative in each instance came from an American official conveys a suggestion of a residue of United States hegemony.

Libertarians have an easy solution to the question of harmonization to overcome arbitrary and uneconomic distortion brought about by differences in national regulation: eliminate all regulation. This seems to me as utopian, or more so, than devising international institutions or rules for the provision of the modicum of international public goods needed in a market system: open markets, a source of goods in acutely short supply in crises, international money, coordinated policies and a lender of last resort. If buyers and sellers of goods and financial assets trade all over the world, moreover, protection of the ignorant from exploitation by the deceitful may be an international public good as well, rather than merely a national one as in the United States. Government is sometimes, nay often, a bumbler, and sometimes even a malfeasant. But it is sometimes needed to protect the weak, to repress wrongdoing and to prevent an occasional bad situation from getting worse. I assume that libertarians are agreed on the necessity of national and international steps to repress terrorism, including the isolation of terrorist asylums. While it is hyperbolic to equate financial malfeasance with terrorism, intergovernmental agreements to punish both seem desirable to me. On a less high-minded and less moral plane, if diverse actions of governments in different countries are not to leave arbitrary incentives to allocate goods and savings, the answer is harmonization of minimal regulation and coordination of policies that will permit integration of markets along Pareto-optimal lines.

Integration

The definition of integration that I espouse follows the law of one price. In one market there is one price, and if there is one price, there is prima facie evidence of one market. This is not universally agreed. Fritz Machlup, for example, defined integration as the division of labor reached under free trade (1977). This is curious at the semantic level, since integration emphasizes oneness and division underlines two-or-moreness.

Larry Neal has undertaken research on security integration in early markets, testing the price of a single security in two markets to determine whether the markets were sufficiently joined by arbitrage to qualify as integrated (1985a, 1985b). The problem is analogous to one that occupied Adam Smith in *The Wealth of Nations* with respect to the exchange of the London pound on the guilder in Amsterdam, which was different in bank money than in common currency (1776 (1937), pp. 445–6). The integration of the market for one money, money spot and forward, or one security in two places may not represent integration of the capital market more generally. For this one needs integration of the markets for a sufficient number of assets so that the broad range of interest rates, and perhaps the profit rates as represented by such measures as the price/earnings ratios, converge. Since the returns on different securities and real assets may be affected by the risk they carry, the criterion for integration of capital markets is generally taken as the relatively riskless return on government securities of the same maturity. To test only this market, however, is incomplete.

National integration of capital markets was achieved slowly in evolutionary fashion in the several centuries to the present, and in different patterns depending upon the nature of the asset. In nineteenth-century France Dijon complained that its lack of banks made it have to pay interest rates of 9 or 10 percent, whereas Paris to the north had rates of 4 percent, and Lyons to the south, awash in fortunes made in silk, enjoyed rates down to 3 percent (Gille, 1970, pp. 57, 77). Sayers tells the story of Lloyds Bank of Birmingham offering a fixed rate to depositors in its home city, but varying the deposit rate to its London customers with the discount rate of the Bank of England, only later to abandon the practice and charge one rate throughout the system when it observed depositors shifting deposits from the London office to Birmingham, or the other way, depending on the rates offered (Sayers, 1957, pp. 110, 165, 270).

Local monopolies gradually broke down as commercial banks in most countries developed national networks, though not in the United States where it was forbidden. Banks starting in areas rich in savings established branches where the demand for loans was brisk; those with excess demands for loans sought out new offices in areas with abundant savings. Economies of scale brought both sets to national financial centers. These economies consisted in greater access to information and the agglomeration effect of centralized shopping for buyers and selling for sellers. Financial centers grew at the expense of regional and local money and capital markets, but did not destroy them completely. In sailing, most of the information needed is available from centrally issued charts from the Geodetic Survey or the Admiralty, but there are some dangers for which one needs local knowledge, and for large ships involving big risks, local pilots. By the same token, there continues to be a need for local banks or bank branches in the provinces and smaller localities on the ground that the London, Paris or New York computers cannot store all the credit and business information, with its subtle shadings, needed for making loans at the local level. Detailed knowledge and face-to-face interchange cannot be dispensed with altogether.

The aggregation that produces major financial centers differs from trade in commodities and from that in finance illustrated by Figure 1. Instead of the excess demand for savings being transferred to the financial center, or the excess supply, as occurs in the early stages of financial development, at advanced levels borrowers and lenders from the smaller center both move their

activity to the metropolitan one, as shown, for example, in
Figure 2. The demand curves are added, and the supply curves,
but beyond the simple addition there is a downward shift in the
supply schedule of savings, as shown in the dotted line. Because
they are acquiring an asset with a wider market, i.e., a more liquid
one, savers are prepared to accept a lower rate of return. The
financial activity can be transferred from the smaller to the
central market because money is almost costless to move. In the
early days of commodity trade goods were relayed from central
entrepôts like Amsterdam and London. With the widespread
diffusion of information on what was needed and available
where, direct trade replaced the indirect to economize on transport costs. But the entrepôts continued to flourish in finance.

With the development of the Euro-currency market, the first
banks to move to, say, London were those of the U.S. money
centers, which went to take an active part in the broadening
market on both sides, borrowing and lending. They were followed
by a number of regional banks which established representation,
not to lend on a significant scale, but to be in a position to borrow
when money was tight in the United States. The Franklin National
Bank, for example, financed its foreign-exchange speculation
with Euro-dollars. In the 1969 "crunch" U.S. regional banks
borrowed dollars in London as an alternative to approaching the

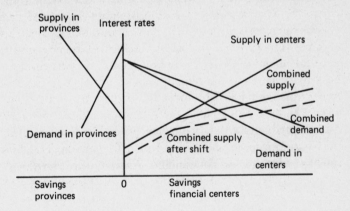

Figure 2. Demand and supply transferred from province to financial
center

tightening Federal funds market, or risking the frowns of the Federal Reserve System by going too frequently to the discount window.

For the capital as opposed to the money market, there has been a distinction between the primary and the secondary market that seems on its way to extinction. The issue hardly arises with bank-syndicated term loans. These are issued on a world-wide basis through syndicates assembled by a lead bank or a group of lead banks which share out the loans to other institutions with which they have close relations. Since there is little trading in these loans after issuance, the question of a secondary market hardly arises, although it has been suggested that a means of assisting with the Third World debt problem would be to develop one. The more pressing problem, however, is for the lead banks to persuade their affiliates to renew the loans when they fall due and cannot be repaid, and to lend more, when some of the smaller and regional banks are regretting their involvement in the first place.

For bonds and large equity issues, particularly such enormous issues as the nationalized companies (British Petroleum and British Telecommunications) being sold off by the Thatcher government, there are similar initial issuing syndicates, world-wide, that underwrite the issue. Subsequent trading has typically taken place in a secondary market with a fixed location, to which buyers and sellers repair to acquire or get rid of a few securities. Before the development of satellite communication and computers, search costs to find the best price for relatively small lots required a central location. The new techniques are now making it possible to gather price information from and to disseminate it to all markets, so that secondary markets are being freed, like primary ones – for widely traded issues at least – from localization. The market for major currencies goes round the world, twenty-four hours a day, with time off on the weekend, from Tokyo to Singapore and Hong Kong, to Bahrein, Frankfurt, London and then New York and Los Angeles, before starting the next day in Tokyo. The same pattern is in formation for the leading securities of the leading countries – to carry out the process of integration of capital markets dimly foreseen by Alfred Marshall almost a century ago.

One curiosum in this story is the wave of interest in capital-market integration that built up in Europe in the 1960s that bore little if any fruit. The Bank for International Settlements' Monetary and Economics Department produced a study on *Capital Markets* (January 1964). An Economic Research Group of a consortium of European banks – the Amsterdam-Rotterdam Bank, the Deutsche Bank, Midland Bank, Société Générale de Banque: General Maatschappij – leading institutions in the Netherlands, West Germany, England, and Belgium respectively, undertook a study entitled *Capital Markets in Europe*, limited, however, to the four countries involved (March 1966). In November of the same year, the Commission of the E.E.C. brought out a report of a group of experts on *The Development of a European Capital Market*, called the Segré report after the chairman of the group, Claudio Segré (1966). In 1967 and 1968, the Committee on Invisible Transactions of the O.E.C.D. produced a five-volume *Capital Markets Study* with statistical appendices. The foci of the separate studies were by no means identical, especially as regards the countries concerned and the emphasis on gathering data, but all were interested in such deviations from competitive and integrated markets as preferences in national markets for governmental borrowers, the limited numbers of foreign securities of companies of European origin quoted on stock exchanges outside their own countries, and the thinness of markets for purely national securities. The reports produced little in the way of action to achieve integration of capital markets at the European level. In my opinion, the failure, if it should be called that, was because European integration was proceeding within a wider framework.

Euro-currency and Euro-bond markets are to a considerable extent misnamed, not only because they stretch around the world, but because they were from the beginning markets that took European borrowers and savers out of Europe. Insofar as integration means convergence of interest rates, European integration has been achieved to some degree, but the mechanism is different from that derived from the ordinary analogy with customs unions for commodities. It is a paradox that integration in the form of the equalization of prices can be achieved between two parties without direct contact with one another, if each is in close contact with the same third party. The banal mathematical statement of the position is that things equal to the same thing are equal to each other. It is legitimate, however, to question whether two markets are integrated if they are not buying and selling directly from and to one another, and this is true for financial assets and labor, as well as commodities. Much of the progress made in European integration since World War II has been achieved through third or outside factors. Mediterranean labor that stood ready to move from France to Germany, or the other way, helped to equate wage rates in Germany and France when few Germans or French, if any, were prepared themselves to work in the other country. If entrepreneurship is admitted as a factor of production, the multinational corporation from the United States, choosing a site for a new investment somewhere in the Common Market, or to a smaller extent, standing ready to shift existing production from one country to another, tended to equalize rates of profits in Europe. By the same token, the return to capital in various European countries was helped to converge by investors buying Euro-currency bonds, and corporations, semi-public bodies and governments selling them in the Euro-market. It is perhaps possible to call this integration when, say, the German and the French capital markets are each regarded as part of a wider entity, including the Euro-currency and -bond markets. If, however, there is only limited financial traffic between the German and French money and capital markets, it is somehow awkward to call them integrated. Factor-price equalization produced by direct contact is readily called integration, as in Figure 3a. The European design suggested in Figure 3b, on a wider level, is perhaps the more normal pattern, involving hierarchical relationships between a center and the satellite areas, much along the lines that prevail within individual countries. It is true that Australia and Canada, and to a lesser degree Japan and the United States, are not dominated by a single financial center to the same extent as London dominates Britain and Paris dominates France. It seems likely that European financial integration will be folded into that of the world, and in hierarchical fashion along the lines of Figure 3b, but without the apex having a specific location.

The Euro-currency markets

The dollar has had an important role in integrating the European capital market, or at least in assisting interest rates to converge. From time to time it has been thought that Europe might develop a currency of its own – the unit of account that was used in the early reckoning of the European Economic Community, or later the European Currency Unit (Ecu). Some experts favored the use of the Special Drawing Right in which the accounts of the International Monetary Fund were kept after the floating of the dollar in 1973, and especially after it had been streamlined to its composition as a weighted average of five leading currencies, rather than the much larger original number. Various banks on occasions have taken the initiative in accepting deposits in units of account, of Ecus, or SDRs, but the attempts have been fitful, limited and I believe ultimately abandoned. As the dollar has weakened as a vehicle currency, the Euro-bond market has increasingly issued Dm, and recently, yen-dominated instruments, but artificial units made up of weighted combinations of actual currencies have failed to catch on.

The reason is that there is a distinct economy in transactions costs in having the same unit used both as medium of exchange and store of value, without the need to undertake an exchange operation when money is spent. The saving does not look enormous; it is nonetheless real. It accounts for the fact that the gold standard inexorably evolved into the gold-exchange standard, to enable the world to make and receive payments in sterling from

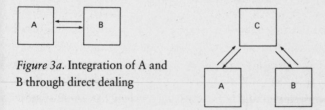

Figure 3a. Integration of A and B through direct dealing

Figure 3b. Integration of A and B through C

Figure 3. Integration through direct interchange and through a third country

roughly 1850 to 1914, and in dollars after World War II. From time to time – with the breakup of the gold pool in 1968, the closing of the gold window in the United States in 1971, the adoption of floating in 1973 – it has appeared that the worldwide use of the dollar as medium of exchange and store of value would be abandoned. Many, including me, predicted it. The beginnings of enhanced financial dealings in Dm and yen have seemed to signal the start of a movement away from dollars. But as in all finance, domestic and international, the economies of scale of a single center, a primary currency, and a substantial number of securities traded in many countries simultaneously are hard to overcome. The dollar may well lose out over the generations ahead. I predict it will not do so to a composite currency but to a national one. The path of the competition will be uneven, with occasional setbacks to various contenders and occasional leaps ahead. For a new world currency to win out over the dollar it must pull far enough ahead of the others to take over the scale economies.

The other major point about the Euro-currency market is its enormous size. Most of this is interbank deposits, rather than loans to and deposits of non-bank debtors and creditors. There is a great deal of borrowing *and* lending by a given non-bank as well, an industrial company for example, borrowing when it plans an investment project and depositing the proceeds back in the Euro-currency market until used. In the past banks in the United States have required borrowers to maintain minimum deposits related to loans. With the deposit earning no interest – before the adoption of Negotiable Orders of Withdrawal or NOW accounts – this was a means of increasing the rate of interest on a loan. A ten percent interest rate on a loan of which twenty percent had to be kept as a compensating balance was in effect a loan of eighty percent of the nominal amount at a 12½ percent interest charge. As far as I see now, however, the present practice of borrowing and lending back by non-banks, both in the United States and in the Euro-currency market, originates largely on the side of the borrower and is a device to provide assured liquidity when needed. The cost is the difference between the borrowing and the deposit rate, which is likely to be narrow for a large multinational company with an excellent credit standing. Just as oil companies undertaking the construction of the Alaska pipeline ordered and took delivery of the pipe when they planned the investment, storing the pipe until needed as insurance against being unable to fill their orders at some later time when steel capacity was stretched, so companies borrow and relend to ensure access to funds for capital expenditure. In the early 1980s, moreover, the Brazilian monetary authorities both kept on borrowing and allowed their foreign-exchange reserves to pile up to several billion dollars. The difference between what was earned on their foreign balances and paid for the loans up to the same amount could be regarded as an insurance premium protecting against the possibility of a sudden halt in new loans at a time when they had no cash on hand.

The vast majority of the funds bought and sold in the Euro-currency market are, as already stated, traded among banks, each trying to settle into a preferred position to feel comfortable with respect to the currencies, terms and credit ratings of both assets and liabilities. In the currency field, for example, a number of banks started out bravely after the adoption of floating accepting the counterpart of their customers' exchange positions, at least for a time to see whether another customer would take an opposite one. This led them to stay long or short of various currencies. With the failures of the Herstatt and Franklin National Banks in 1974, however, most banks moved to close out open currency positions, usually daily, and sometimes even within the day. A considerable amount of the churning in the market is the passing on of open positions contracted in dealing with customers to another bank with perhaps an opposite need. Most of it is to settle into more comfortable because less risky positions regarding debtor-creditor standings and the term structure of assets and liabilities. Interbank trading is undertaken for tiny commissions, but is profitable because of the enormous amounts turned over. These huge interbank dealings are associated with relatively small net changes with the outside world.

The roads ahead

The vast sums traded in Euro-currency markets and moving daily round the world are nervous-making. World wealth has increased on an impressive scale since 1950 and the ratio of liquid assets to wealth has risen. The amount of liquid assets is hence enormous, and such liquid assets can readily be redirected from one accustomed habitat to other currencies, banks and/or financial centers in response to changes in market psychology. If savers and investors made up their minds independently, some optimistic, some pessimistic about prospects here and there, the threat would not be so great as average outcomes would yield stability. To the extent that market participants are tuned in to the same information and forecasts on a world scale, and closely observe each other's actions, wide changes of opinion become possible and with them large international movements of funds. As noted earlier, before World War II, an enormous run on a national currency involved as much as $100 million a day. In the 1980s, a similar shock can produce movements running to several billion dollars a day. If world events are occasionally alarming and world financial opinion occasionally fickle, the roads ahead look fraught with dangers.

Two outcomes are possible. One is the gradual uneven development of world finance into the kind of integrated single market, with a single world money, a single world money market, a single world capital market, and a single world monetary policy. Differences from the world monetary policy and adjustments of fiscal policy would be undertaken in separate countries to trim national direction when it veered too far away from the world direction. The pattern to be achieved would be similar to the integration of money and capital markets, and the common monetary policy, within the United States, with national central banks playing roles only slightly more important than those of the separate Federal Reserve Banks outside of New York. Savings would be gathered in the world financial network, largely from the richer countries, but also from rich people in the poorer ones, and distributed to those countries (or rather those businesses in all countries) where the marginal productivity of capital was high, whether because of local scarcity of capital due to poverty and inadequate savings, or because of rapid growth and surging innovation. Aging rich countries will doubtless consume capital while the nouveaux riches accumulate it in substantial amount. The regional patterns within the United States offer a further analogy, with the thrusting Sunbelt, and innovative areas such as California and the high-tech area around Boston borrowing on balance from the rest of the country despite high incomes and high savings. The poorer parts of the country such as Northern New England and the Mississippi delta borrow. The Smokestack area in the Middle West consumes wealth on balance. But the amount of buying and selling of securities, and movement of money – national rather than international capital movements – are enormous on a gross basis, much less impressive net.

The analogy between a country and an integrated world of sovereign states fails at the level of transfers. National governments operate through budgets that raise revenue on one regional basis and spend it on another, even when the budget is balanced and produces no net movement of capital regionally. (Separate regions, to be sure, may experience net capital flows through the government debt when there is no change in the total, as refunding operations have different impacts in different regions.) Where taxes are progressive and social expenditure favors the poor, the regional transfers through the fisc can be substantial. In the international field, on the contrary, contributions to common budgets such as regional defense in N.A.T.O., A.N.Z.U.S. and A.S.E.A.N., or disbursements of such international bodies as the United Nations, the specialized agencies, the I.M.F., I.B.R.D. and the regional development banks, plus other multilateral and all bilateral aid are not so great as to contribute significantly to balance-of-payments adjustment among nations. The analogy is further faulted by the responsibility of national government, missing in the international sphere, for providing the public goods of full employment, equitable income distribution, macro-economic stability and disaster relief. Comparable public goods at the international level are much more difficult to provide even with a hegemonic system. As the economic dominance of the United States declines, some political scientists believe that such public goods can be provided by "regimes," or institutionalized habits of cooperation begun under the hegemonic structure (Keohane, 1984). The question is debated, and unresolved.

The alternate road to the gradual federalization of macro-economic behavior on a world basis (excluding the Socialist bloc) is one of decoupling, self-reliance, autarky, as recommended in some parts of the Third World. The rationale is largely leftist today but chapter and verse as a text for the position can be found in J. M. Keynes' *Yale Review* article "National Self-Sufficiency," written in a dark mood at the depth of the depression (1933, p. 758):

Ideas, knowledge, science, hospitality, travel – these are the things which should of their nature be international. But let goods be homespun whenever it is reasonable and conveniently possible, and above all let finance be primarily national.

"Primarily" takes some of the sting out of the "above all," and Keynes himself had recovered to an international position by the end of the war (1946). The Third World debt crisis of the 1980s finds few countries prepared to take the decoupling road, no matter how much they call for a New International Economic Order. But the seed remains in the ground and may sprout if the world disintegrates economically as it did in the 1930s.

One strong possibility is that the world proceeds to disintegrate in the field of trade – witness, for example, the difficulties with the Japanese export surplus that stubbornly refuses to melt, the trade war brewing between the United States and the Common Market over the diversion of Spanish and Portuguese food imports from the United States to Europe after Spain and Portugal join the Market, not to mention the problem of finding outlets for Third World industrial exports, in regulating trade in services, and in containing non-trade barriers, or N.T.B.s – all this at the time when integration is proceeding in finance, *faute de mieux*, because it is impossible to restrain money in a world of modern communication. Trade and finance have been linked many times. Finance followed trade, for example, in Venice, Bruges, Antwerp, Amsterdam, Hamburg and London. Occasionally the two functions have gone different ways, as trade shifted from entrepôt operations to direct relations to save transport costs, while finance kept to the domination of a single center with its economies of scale, since the cost of moving money is not substantial. If the world of trade were to disintegrate, while that of finance remains integrated because money is so hard to contain, governments would be hard put to determine the appropriate degree of operation in one sphere and discord in another.

One lesson seems clear: that the difficulty of damming money flows in separate countries will require cooperation, achieved with intermittent gains and setbacks, in surveillance of money and capital markets when disturbed, and ultimately in the coordination of monetary and fiscal policies. It would be tragic if the world could not be kept open for the movement of goods, services and people too. More important than the maintenance of open markets for goods, however, are the tasks of macro-economic coordination, dampening excited movements of exchange rates, and maintaining an international lender of last resort for meeting crises.

References

Aftalion, Albert (1927), *Monnaie, prix et change*, Paris: Sirey.

Akiyama, Taro and Yusuke Onitsuka (1985), "Current account, capital exports and optimal patterns of developmental stages of balance of payments," Discussion Paper Series 85–7, Center for International Trade Studies, Faculty of Economics, Yokohama National University.

Alexander, Sidney S. (1952), "Effect of a devaluation on a trade balance," *Staff Papers*, vol. 2 (April), pp. 263–78.

Aliber, Robert Z. (1970), "A theory of direct foreign investment," in C. P. Kindleberger, ed., *The International Corporation*, Cambridge, Mass.: M.I.T. Press, pp. 17–34.

   (1983), "Money, multinationals and sovereigns," in C. P. Kindleberger and D. B. Audretch, eds., *The Multinational Corporation in the 1980s*, Cambridge, Mass.: M.I.T. Press, pp. 245–59.

Bagehot, Walter (1978), *The Collected Works of Walter Bagehot* edited by N. St John-Stevas, London: the *Economist*.

Bank for International Settlements (1964), *Capital Markets*, C. B. 333, Basle.

Bennett, Edward W. (1962), *Germany and the Diplomacy of the Financial Crisis, 1931*, Cambridge, Mass.: Harvard University Press.

Beyen, J. W. (1949), *Money in a Maelstrom*, New York: Macmillan.

Bouvier, Jean (1960), *Le Krach de l'Union Générale, 1878–1885*, Paris: Presses Universitaires de France.

Bullock, C. J., J. H. Williams, and R. S. Tucker (1919), "The balance of trade of the United States," in *Review of Economics and Statistics*, July.

Cairncross, Sir Alec (1953), *Home and Foreign Investment, 1870–1913*, Cambridge: Cambridge University Press.

Checkland, S. G. (1975), *Scottish Banking: A History, 1695–1973*, Glasgow: Collins.

Chevalier, Michel (1867) in Ministère des Finances et Ministère de l'Agriculture, du commerce et des Travaux, *Enquête sur les principles et les faits généraux qui régissent la circulation monétaire et fiduciare*, 6 vols. Paris: Imprimerie Impériale.

(Coats, R. H.) (1915), Board of Inquiry into cost of living (1915), *Report of the Board*, two vols, Ottawa.

Confalonieri, Antonio (1976), *Banca e industria in Italia*, 3 vols, Milan: Banca Commerciale Italiana.

Coombs, Charles A. (1976), *The Arena of International Finance*, New York: Wiley-Interscience.

Cooper, Richard N. (1984), "Is there a need for reform?" in *The International Monetary System: Forty Years after Bretton Woods*, Federal Reserve Bank of Boston, Conference Series No. 28, pp. 21–39.

Corbo, Vittorio and Jaime De Melo (1985), "Liberalization with stabilization in the Southern Cone of Latin America," Special Issue of *World Development*, vol. 13, No. 8 (August).

Day, John (1978), "The great bullion famine of the fifteenth century," *Past and Present*, No. 79, pp. 3–54.

Debeir, Jean Claude (1978), "La crise du franc de 1924: un exemple de spéculation 'internationale,' " *Relations internationales*, No. 13, pp. 29–49.

(1982), "Comment," on Carl-L. Holtfrerich, "Domestic and foreign expectations and the demand for money during the German inflation, 1920–1923," in C. P. Kindleberger and J.-P. Leffargue, eds., *Financial Crises: Theory, History and Policy*, Cambridge: Cambridge University Press, pp. 132–6.

de Roover, Raymond (1949), *Gresham on Foreign Exchange: An Essay on Early English Mercantilism*, Cambridge, Mass.: Harvard University Press.

Despres, Emile, C. P. Kindleberger, and W. S. Salant (1966), "The dollar and world liquidity: a minority view," in the *Economist*, vol. 218, No. 6380 (February 5).

Diaz Alejandro, Carlos F. (1985), "Goodbye financial repression; hello financial crash," *Journal of Economic Development*, (December).

Dollinger, Philippe (1964 (1970)), *The German Hansa*, Stanford, Cal.: Stanford University Press.

Economic Research Group of Amsterdam-Rotterdam Bank, Deutsche Bank, Midland Bank, Société Générale de Banque-Generale Bankmaatschappij (1966), *Capital Markets in Europe: A Study of*

Markets in Belgium, West Germany, the Netherlands and the United Kingdom, no place stated.

Einzig, Paul (1937, 2nd edn, 1967), *A Dynamic Theory of Forward Exchange*, London: Macmillan.

Emden, Paul (1938), *Money Powers of the Nineteenth and Twentieth Centuries*, New York: Appleton-Century.

European Economic Community, Commission (1966), *The Development of a European Capital Market, Report of a Group of Experts Appointed by the EEC Commission*, Brussels, European Economic Community.

Ferns, H. S. (1960), *Britain and Argentina in the Nineteenth Century*, Oxford: Clarendon Press.

Flannery, Mark J., and Jack M. Guttentag (1980), "Problem banks: examination, identification and supervision," in Leonard Lapidus *et al.*, *State and Federal Regulation of Commercial Banks*, Washington, D.C., Federal Deposit Insurance Corporation, vol. II, pp. 171–226.

Gerschenkron, Alexander (1962), *Economic Backwardness in Historical Perspective, A Book of Essays*, Cambridge, Mass.: Belnap Press of Harvard University Press.

Gille, Bertrand (1970), *La banque en France au XIX siècle: recherches historiques*, Geneva: Droz.

Goldsmith, Raymond W. (1969), *Financial Structure and Development*, New Haven: Yale University Press.

Gowa, Joanne (1983), *Closing the Gold Window: Domestic Politics and the End of Bretton Woods*, Ithaca and London: Cornell University Press.

Hall, A. B. (1963), *The London Capital Market and Australia, 1870–1914*, Canberra: A.N.U. Social Science Monograph, No. 2.

Harley, C. Knick (1977), "The interest rate and prices in Britain, 1873–1913: a study of the Gibson paradox," *Explorations in Economic History*, vol. 14, pp. 69–89.

Hayek, Friedrich A. (1972), *Choice in Currency: A Way to Stop Inflation*, Institute of Economic Affairs Occasional Papers, No. 48, London: I.E.A.

Heckscher, Eli F. (1931 (1953)), "Natural and money economy, as illustrated from Swedish history in the sixteenth century," in F. C. Lane and J. C. Riersma, eds., *Enterprise and Secular Change: Readings in Economic History*, Homewood, Ill.: Irwin, pp. 206–28.

Henry, James S. (1986), "Third World debt hoax: where the money went," in *The New Republic*, vol. 37, no. 17, pp. 20–3.

Hirschman, Albert O. (1969), "How to divest in Latin America and why," *Essays in International Finance*, No. 76 (November), Princeton, N.J.: International Finance Section, Princeton University.

Holtfrerich, Carl-Ludwig (1980), *Die deutsche Inflation, 1914–23*, Berlin: Walter de Gruyter.

(1982), "Domestic and foreign expectations and the demand for money during the German inflation, 1920–1923," in C. P. Kindleberger and J.-P. Laffargue, eds., *Financial Crises: Theory, History and Policy*, Cambridge: Cambridge University Press, pp. 117–32.

Hymer, Stephen H. (1960 (1976)), *The International Operations of National Firms: A Study of Direct Foreign Investment*, Cambridge, Mass.: M.I.T. Press.

Ingram, James C. (1959), "State and Regional Payments Mechanism," in *Quarterly Journal of Economics*, vol. 73, no. 4, pp. 619–32.

International Bank for Reconstruction and Development (1949), Press release no. 134, May 11.

Israelsen, L. Dwight (1979), "The determinants of Russian state income, 1800–1914: an econometric analysis," Ph.D. dissertation, Massachusetts Institute of Technology.

Jefferys, J. B. (1938 (1977)), "Trends in Business Organization in Great Britain" (Ph.D. dissertation, London School of Economics; published New York: Arno Press).

(1946 (1954)), "The denomination and character of shares, 1855–1885," in E. M. Carus-Wilson, ed., *Essays in Economic History*, vol. 1, London: Edward Arnold, pp. 344–57.

Johnson, Harry G. (1971), "The efficiency and welfare implications of the international corporation," in C. P. Kindleberger, ed., *The International Corporation*, Cambridge, Mass.: M.I.T. Press, pp. 35–56.

Keohane, Robert O. (1984), *After Hegemony: Cooperation and Discord in the World Political Economy*, Princeton, N.J.: Princeton University Press.

Keynes, J. Maynard (1924), *Tract on Monetary Reform*, London: Macmillan.

(1929), "The German transfer problem," *Economic Journal*, vol. 39, no. 1, pp. 1–7.

(1930), *Treatise on Money*, New York: Harcourt Brace.

(1933), "National self-sufficiency," *Yale Review*, vol. 22, no. 4 (June).

(1936), *The General Theory of Employment, Interest and Money*, New York: Harcourt Brace.

(1946), "The Balance of Payments of the United States," *Economic Journal*, vol. 56 (June), pp. 172–87.

Kindleberger, Charles P. (1963 (1966)), "European integration and the development of a single financial center for long-term capital,"

Weltwirtschaftliches Archiv, Band 90, Heft 2, pp. 189–209, reprinted in idem, *Europe and the Dollar*, Cambridge, Mass.: M.I.T. Press, pp. 62–83.

(1969 (1981)), "Measuring equilibrium in the balance of payments," *Journal of Political Economy*, vol. 77, no. 6, pp. 873–91, reprinted in idem, *International Money*, London: George Allen & Unwin, pp. 120–38.

(1975 (1981)), "Quantity and price, especially in financial markets," *Quarterly Review of Economics and Business*, vol. 15, no. 2, pp. 7–19, reprinted in idem, *International Money*, London: George Allen & Unwin, pp. 256–68.

(1978a), *Manias, Panics and Crashes, A History of Financial Crises*, New York: Basic Books.

(1978b), *Economic Response: Comparative Studies in Trade, Finance and Growth*, Cambridge, Mass.: Harvard University Press.

(1984), *A Financial History of Western Europe*, London: George Allen & Unwin.

(1985a), *Keynesianism vs. Monetarism and Other Essays in Financial History*, London: George Allen & Unwin.

(1985b), "Bank failures: the 1930s and the 1980s," in *The Search for Financial Stability: The Past Fifty Years*, A conference sponsored by the Federal Reserve Bank of San Francisco, pp. 7–34.

(1985c), "Multinational enterprise: unit or agglomeration?" in Toshio Shisjido and Ryuzo Sato, eds., *Economic Policy and Development: New Perspectives*, Dover, Mass.: Auburn House, pp. 33–45.

Kogut, Bruce (1983), "Foreign direct investment as a sequential process," in C. P. Kindleberger and D. B. Audretch, eds., *The Multinational Corporation in the 1980s*, Cambridge, Mass.: M.I.T. Press, pp. 38–56.

Koszul, Julien-Pierre (1971), "American banks in Europe," in C. P. Kindleberger, ed., *The International Corporation: A Symposium*, Cambridge, Mass.: M.I.T. Press, pp. 273–89.

Lamfalussy, Alexandre (1961), *Investment and Growth in Mature Economies: The Case of Belgium*, London: Macmillan.

(1985), "The changing environment of Central Bank policy," *American Economic Review*, vol. 75, no. 2, pp. 409–13.

Lauck, W. Jett (1907), *The Causes of the Panic of 1893*, Boston: Houghton Mifflin.

League of Nations (Ragnar Nurkse) (1944), "International currency experience: lessons of the interwar period," Princeton, N.J.: League of Nations.

Machlup, Fritz (1950 (1964)), "Three concepts of so-called dollar shortage," *Economic Journal*, vol. 60, no. 1, pp. 46–8, reprinted in idem, *International Payments, Debts and Gold*, New York: Scribners, pp. 110–35.

(1958 (1964)), "Equilibrium and disequilibrium: misplaced concreteness and disguised politics," *Economic Journal*, LXIII (March), pp. 10–24, reprinted in idem, *International Payments Debts, and Gold*, New York: Scribners, pp. 11–39.

(1977), *A History of Thought on Economic Integration*, London: Macmillan.

(1980), "My early work in international monetary problems," Banca Nazionale del Lavoro *Quarterly Review*, no. 133 (June), pp. 113–46.

Marshall, Alfred (1930), *Principles of Economics: An Introductory Volume*, 8th edn, London: Macmillan.

(1923 (1960)), *Money, Credit and Commerce*, New York: A. M. Kelley (reprints of Economic Classics).

McKinnon, Ronald I. (1973), *Money and Capital in Economic Development*, Washington, D.C.: The Brookings Institution.

(1982), "The order of economic liberalization: lessons from Chile and Argentina," in K. Brunner and H. Netzer, eds., *Economic Policy in a World of Change*, Amsterdam: North-Holland.

, and Donald J. Mathieson (1981), "How to manage a repressed economy," *Essays in International Finance*, No. 145 (December), Princeton, N.J.: International Finance Section.

Morgenstern, Oskar (1959), *International Financial Transactions and Business Cycles*, Princeton, N.J.: Princeton University Press.

Mundell, Robert A. (1968), "Testimony," before Republican balance-of-payments seminar, Congressional Record, February 6.

Neal, Larry (1985a), "Integration of international capital markets: quantitative evidence from the eighteenth to the twentieth centuries," *Journal of Economic Literature*, vol. 45, no. 2 (June), pp. 219–26.

(1985b), "Integration and efficiency of the London and Amsterdam stock markets in the eighteenth century," Faculty Working Paper No. 1177, Bureau of Economic Research, University of Illinois (September).

Norton, R. D. (1986), "Industrial policy and American renewal," *Journal of Economic Literature*, vol. 44, no. 1 (March), pp. 1–40.

Nurkse, Ragnar (1949), "Conditions of international monetary equilibrium," in American Economic Association, *Readings in the Theory of International Trade*, Philadelphia: Blakiston, pp. 1–18.

Olson, Mancur (1982), *The Rise and Decline of Nations: Economic Growth, Stagflation and Social Rigidities*, New Haven: Yale University Press.

Organization of Economic Cooperation and Development, Committee for Invisible Transactions (1967, 1968), *Capital Markets Study*, five vols.

Pedersen, Jørgen (1933, 1934) in League of Nations *Sixth International Studies Conference*, a record of a second study conference on "A state and economic life," May 26 to June 2, 1953, Paris: International Institute of Intellectual Cooperation.

Platt, D. C. M. (1984), *Foreign Finance in Continental Europe and the USA, 1815–1870: Quantities, Origins, Functions and Distribution*, London: George Allen & Unwin.

Postan, M. M. (1973), *Medieval Trade and Finance*, Cambridge: Cambridge University Press.

Review Committee for the Balance of Payments Statistics to the U.S. Bureau of the Budget (1965), *The Balance of Payments of the United States, A Review and Appraisal*, Washington, D.C.: Government Printing Office.

Robertson, Sir Dennis H. (1953), *Britain in the World Economy*, London: George Allen & Unwin.

Salant, Walter S. (1966), "Capital markets and the balance of payments of a financial center," in W. Fellner, F. Machlup and R. Triffin, eds., *Maintaining and Restoring Balance in International Payments*, Princeton, N.J.: Princeton University Press, pp. 177–96.

Sayers, R. S. (1957), *Lloyds Bank in the History of English Banking*, Oxford: Clarendon.

Segré, Claudio (1966), *Segré Report*, see European Economic Community.

Shaw, Edward S. (1973), *Financial Deepening in Economic Development*, New York: Oxford University Press.

Siegel, Barry N. (1984), *Money in Crisis: The Federal Reserve, the Economy, and Monetary Reform*, Cambridge, Mass.: Ballinger Press (for the Pacific Institute for Public Policy Research).

Simon, Matthew (1955 (1978)), *Cyclical Fluctuations and the International Capital Movements of the United States, 1865–1897*, New York: Arno Press.

Smith, Adam (1887 (1937)), *An Inquiry into the Nature and Causes of the Wealth of Nations*, ed. E. Cannon, New York: Modern Library.

Spero, Joan Edelman (1980), *The Failure of the Franklin National Bank: Challenge to the International Banking System*, New York: Columbia University Press (for the Council on Foreign Relations).

Sprague, O. M. W. (1910), *History of Crises under the National Banking System*, Washington, D.C.: Government Printing Office, for the National Monetary Commission.

Stern, Fritz (1977), *Gold and Iron: Bismarck, Bleichroder and the Building of the German Empire*, London: George Allen & Unwin.

Strange, Susan (1976), *International Monetary Relations*, vol. 2 of Andrew Shonfield, ed., *International Economic Relations of the Western World*, London: Oxford University Press.

Timberlake, Richard H. J. *et al.* (1985), "The deregulation of banking in the United States", a symposium presented at the American Economic Association, December 28–30 1984, in *American Economic Review*, vol. 75, no. 2 (May) *Papers and Proceedings*, pp. 97–113.

Triffin, Robert (1958), *Gold and the Dollar Crisis*, New Haven: Yale University Press.

Vaubel, Roland (1977), "Free currency competition," *Weltwirtschaftliches Archiv*, vol. 113, pp. 435–59.

(1984), "The government's money monopoly: externalities or natural monopoly?" *Kyklos*, vol. 37, no. 1, pp. 27–58.

Viner, Jacob (1924), *Canada's Balance of International Indebtedness, 1900–1913: An Inductive Study of the Theory of International Trade*, Cambridge, Mass.: Harvard University Press.

(1952), *International Economics*, Glencoe, Ill.: Free Press.

Wallich, Henry C. (1984a), "Why is net international investment so small?" in Wolfram Engels, Armin Gutowski and Henry C. Wallich, eds., *International Capital Movements, Debt and Monetary System*, Mainz: v. Hase & Koehler, pp. 417–37.

(1984b), "International capital movements: the tail that wags the dog," in *The International Monetary System: Forty Years after Bretton Woods*, Federal Reserve Bank of Boston, Conference Series No. 28, pp. 179–87.

White, Lawrence H. (1983), "Competitive monies, inside and out," *Cato Journal*, vol. 3 (Spring), pp. 281–99.

(1984), *Free Banking in Britain: Theory, Experience and Debate, 1800–1845*, New York: Cambridge University Press.

Williamson, Jeffery G. (1964), *American Growth and the Balance of Payments, 1820–1913: A Study of the Long Swing*, Chapel Hill: University of North Carolina Press.

Williamson, John, ed. (1983), *IMF Conditionality*, Washington, D.C.: Institute for International Economics.

Index